Samuel French Acting Edition

Will Success Spoil Rock Hunter?

by George Axelrod

SAMUELFRENCH.COM   SAMUELFRENCH.CO.UK

Copyright © 1955 (as an unpublished work) by George Axelrod
Copyright © 1956, 1957 (acting edition) by George Axelrod
All Rights Reserved

WILL SUCCESS SPOIL ROCK HUNTER? is fully protected under the copyright laws of the United States of America, the British Commonwealth, including Canada, and all other countries of the Copyright Union. All rights, including professional and amateur stage productions, recitation, lecturing, public reading, motion picture, radio broadcasting, television and the rights of translation into foreign languages are strictly reserved.

ISBN 978-0-573-61795-9

www.SamuelFrench.com
www.SamuelFrench.co.uk

For Production Enquiries

United States and Canada
Info@SamuelFrench.com
1-866-598-8449

United Kingdom and Europe
Plays@SamuelFrench.co.uk
020-7255-4302

Each title is subject to availability from Samuel French, depending upon country of performance. Please be aware that *WILL SUCCESS SPOIL ROCK HUNTER?* may not be licensed by Samuel French in your territory. Professional and amateur producers should contact the nearest Samuel French office or licensing partner to verify availability.

CAUTION: Professional and amateur producers are hereby warned that *WILL SUCCESS SPOIL ROCK HUNTER?* is subject to a licensing fee. Publication of this play(s) does not imply availability for performance. Both amateurs and professionals considering a production are strongly advised to apply to Samuel French before starting rehearsals, advertising, or booking a theatre. A licensing fee must be paid whether the title(s) is presented for charity or gain and whether or not admission is charged. Professional/Stock licensing fees are quoted upon application to Samuel French.

No one shall make any changes in this title(s) for the purpose of production. No part of this book may be reproduced, stored in a retrieval system, or transmitted in any form, by any means, now known or yet to be invented, including mechanical, electronic, photocopying, recording, videotaping, or otherwise, without the prior written permission of the publisher. No one shall upload this title(s), or part of this title(s), to any social media websites.

For all enquiries regarding motion picture, television, and other media rights, please contact Samuel French.

Please refer to page 80 for further copyright information.

WILL SUCCESS SPOIL ROCK HUNTER?

was first presented by Jule Styne
at the Belasco Theatre on the evening
of October 13, 1955 with the following cast:

RITA MARLOWE	*Jayne Mansfield*
MASSEUR	*Lew Gallo*
GEORGE MACCAULEY	*Orson Bean*
MICHAEL FREEMAN	*Walter Matthau*
IRVING LASALLE	*Martin Gabel*
HARRY KAYE	*Harry Clark*
A SECRETARY	*Carol Grace*
BRONK BRANNIGAN	*William Thourlby*

Staged by GEORGE AXELROD

Production designed by OLIVER SMITH

Lighting by PEGGY CLARK

Production stage manager PAT CHANDLER

SYNOPSIS OF SCENES

ACT ONE

The sitting room of Rita Marlowe's suite in the St. Regis Hotel in New York City.

A winter morning.

ACT TWO

The office of Rita Marlowe Productions in Hollywood.

Four weeks later.

ACT THREE

SCENE 1: *The Office. An evening, one year later.*

SCENE 2: *The Office. Next morning.*

Will Success Spoil Rock Hunter?

ACT ONE

The curtain rises on the sitting room of RITA MARLOWE'S *suite at the St. Regis Hotel in New York City.*

The room is elegant and old-fashioned and the suite itself is the most expensive in the hotel. (It is interesting to note that there is not a character in this play who would be caught dead in a hotel room that cost less than fifty bucks a day. This suite costs considerably more. But what the hell—it's deductable.)

Through the window we can see New York at its grayest, coldest and gloomiest.

It is late February and the streets are covered with gray slush which will probably freeze by nightfall. The elevator boys all have colds.

This suite, however, is rather cozy. A fire burns in the marble fireplace. The joint looks lived in. That is to say: MISS MARLOWE *has been here for three days and certain evidences of her personality are present. Scattered about are a number of furry toy animals, flowers, cigarette butts, vodka bottles and a genuinely definitive collection of movie and confidential-type magazines.*

The only piece of furniture in the room that is under a hundred years old is a portable, collapsible

massage table on which, at this moment, RITA MAR-
LOWE, *vaguely covered by a towel, is being worked
on by a large, muscular young man in a white T-
shirt.*

You've seen RITA *on the screen so there is no
particular point in describing her here. Except, perhaps, to note that in person she is even more so.*

*The TELEPHONE is ringing during the blackness
before the rise of the curtain.*

RITA. Get it, will you, Honey?

(MASSEUR *hands her phone.*)

(Into phone) Hello! Yes! Just divoon, thank you! Right now? I'm having a massage. You see, I'm getting just a little heavy around the old hipsville and the man at the health club thought that if we could once break down these kind of fatty tissues I have in the upper thighs, it might help. Otherwise I know the studio is going to make me wear one of those terrible elastic girdles and you know I just can't wear elastic next to the skin—especially there. You see, I break out in this kind of a rash—which is very painful and you can't take hot baths or anything so I thought I'd better have a massage. By the way—*who's calling please?*

Oh, yes. They told me. Won't you come right up! *(She hands him phone)* It's some man from one of the movie magazines. He wants to interview me. It won't bother *you,* will it?

MASSEUR. *(Takes phone to table up Right)* Not at all, Miss Marlowe. We're almost finished.

RITA. *(Hands him cigarette)* Because this is the only time I can squeeze him in. I'm having lunch across the street in a little while—and I'm flying back to California tonight for some retakes. After that, as soon as the script is ready, I start NO HIDING PLACE DOWN HERE. Did you see it—it's a play?

MASSEUR. No, I didn't, Miss Marlowe—

RITA. *(Sits up)* Well, it's about this head-doctor who falls in love with kind of a prostitute. Me. And *he* analyses

her and *she analyses* him and it turns out he's a little on the *gaysville* side—on account of his mother—so anyway, they destroy each other. Oh, it's a hell of a thing—and talk about *dirty!* Oh it won the Pulitzer Prize, though. Michael Freeman wrote it. He's the one taking me to lunch. With Mr. Kaye. He's the head of the studio.
　(Door BUZZER.)
Come on in! The door's open!

(GEORGE MACCAULEY *enters Left; closes door. He is a very nervous, rather foolish young man with a crew haircut and a row of pens and pencils in his breast pocket. He wears a Chesterfield overcoat and homburg. He should never be permitted to wear a homburg.)*

　GEORGE. How do you do? I'm Mr. MacCauley. *George* MacCauley. I'm from *MOVIE WORLD.*
　RITA. They told me.
　GEORGE. *(Puts his hat on up Left corner of couch and coat over arm of couch)* I'm certainly very excited about this, Miss Marlowe. *(Takes book out of pocket; looks for pencil)* I mean if it wasn't that Margot Ballantine—she's the *regular* interviewer—well, if she hadn't gotten this kind of food poisoning—I never would have had a chance to write this interview or get to meet you. *(Crosses down Right)* You don't know how exciting it is for me to really see Rita Marlowe, in the *(Turns to her)* flesh— *(As he finds himself staring at a considerable amount of* RITA MARLOWE *in the flesh, he breaks off in embarrassment. Crosses Left)* Maybe it would be better if I waited outside until you finish your—rub down.
　RITA. No, no, no! You stay right here. *He* doesn't mind—do you?
　MASSEUR. Not at all, Miss Marlowe—
　RITA. Sure. You go right over there. Sit down.
　GEORGE. *(Sits on stool Right)* Thank you very much.
　RITA. *(Sits up; faces* GEORGE*)* Now then, what are you going to write, Mr. McCarthy?

GEORGE. *MacCauley*. George MacCauley. Actually, I'm not too experienced. The only other big star I've ever interviewed was Rock Hunter. It was a pretty good interview, though. I called it: WILL SUCCESS SPOIL ROCK HUNTER? Actually, it was very well received. For what it was—

RITA. *(Far away)* You all start out by saying you want to write about the *real* me. The Rita Marlowe that nobody knows— *(To* GEORGE) the shy, lonely girl I really am. But then you always end up by writing the same old things. How I don't wear underpants. My divorce. What I said about the producer—

GEORGE. What did you say about the producer? *(His pencil is poised.)*

RITA. Well, I had an appointment with this producer —he's supposed to be a very famous wolf. And somebody said: "Rita, you must be careful. You get in there alone with that guy and he'll tear the dress right off your back!" So I said: *(Laughs)* "Okay. So I'll wear an old dress!" *(She looks at* GEORGE. *No reaction.)*

GEORGE. *(Pause)* Well, I think that's very sensible.

RITA. *(On stomach)* Don't bother to write it down. Wilson already used it. It was one of Earl's Pearls. *(Crosses legs)* Anyway, Mr. McClure—I was thinking— I was hoping that maybe you'd write a story called: WILL RITA MARLOWE FIND HAPPINESS AGAIN?

GEORGE. "WILL RITA MARLOWE FIND HAPPINESS AGAIN"? Yes, yes. I think that's very interesting.

RITA. Well, Honey, of course it's interesting. Even to me.

GEORGE. Yes.

(Door BUZZER.)

RITA. *(Clockwise roll onto stomach)* Would you answer that, please?

GEORGE. Surely. *(He rises and opens the door, admitting* MICHAEL FREEMAN.)

(MIKE *is a tall, dark-haired rather attractive man in his middle thirties. He is hatless and wears a handsome polo coat. It is just possible that he has stopped at the King Cole Bar downstairs for a couple of quick ones with the newspaper boys.*)

RITA. Michael!
MIKE. *(Crosses to Right Center)* Baby! How are you? *(Kisses her.)*
RITA. *(Turns around on her back)* Divoon, Michael! Absolutely divoon!
   (GEORGE *crosses to Left Center.*)
I want you to meet Michael Freeman—the playwright. Michael, this is Mr. Carstairs—from *PHOTOPLAY*—
GEORGE. MacCauley. From *MOVIE WORLD*.
MIKE. Pleasure.
RITA. Michael is the one you should really be writing the story about. I know you've probably seen his play—
GEORGE. No, actually I haven't. I tried to get tickets for my Aunt's birthday—but they're sold out till next August—
RITA. I think Michael is the most intelligent man I know—and I'm just queer for intelligent men. You know that's true, Michael—I'm absolutely queer for you.
   (MIKE *removes coat.*)
He thinks I'm just buttering up to him because I want to be in the picture. But that's not true. *(To* MIKE—*cute)* I'm going to buy his play so I don't even care whether he likes me or not.
   (GEORGE *writes this down.*)
The studio is paying for it, of course. But *I'm* buying it. Rita Marlowe Incorporated. Oh I didn't tell you, Mr. Casey. I'm the head of my own company now—aren't I, Michael?
MIKE. Well—the titular head— *(Crosses up Right, then down to mantlepiece; takes lighter; lights cigarette.)*
RITA. *(Coldly)* I don't know why some people think it is so cute to start talking dirty in front of the press— Anyway—you better sit down, Mr. McClure.

(GEORGE *sits on couch.*)
I can only give you a few more minutes because Michael and Mr. Kaye—he's the head of the studio—are going to take me across the street to the Pavillion for lunch. To talk about me being in the movie of Michael's play. Mr. Kelly is doing a wonderful story about me, Michael. It's going to be called: WILL RITA MARLOWE FIND HAPPINESS AGAIN?

MIKE. *(Crosses to Left Center)* That sounds pretty rooty-tooty all right—hey look—you got a drink around this joint someplace?

RITA. That's a very good idea— I told you he was intelligent, didn't I? Why don't you make a drink for all of us. I'm just queer for vodka martunis. Oh, you'd like a little vodka martuni, wouldn't you, Mr. Carson?

GEORGE. *(Rises)* Oh, no thank you, thank you, no.

RITA. Oh come on, now don't be a big fat drip!

(GEORGE *sits.*)
You just go ahead and make us all a nice vodka martuni, Michael.

(MIKE *crosses Left to bar.*)
Everything's over there on the bar. But make it very dry—

MIKE. Oh don't worry, baby. 86 to 1.

RITA. *(To* GEORGE) Now where was I?

GEORGE. I don't know, exactly—

RITA. I do. I was going to tell you why I'm so unhappy. Well, the reason I'm so unhappy is that I'm misunderstood. They write so many untrue things about me. They say I don't wear any underwear. Well—of course I wear underwear! In the *winter*. I mean how do they think I hold my stockings up?

GEORGE. *(Pause)* It certainly poses a very interesting problem—

RITA. Of course in the summer I don't wear stockings— so that's different. But in the winter I wear *suspants*.

MIKE. *(Over his shoulder—from the bar)* You can write that down if you want to—

RITA. That's right. Suspants. S-U-S-P-A-N-T-S— It's a kind of panty-girdle—
MIKE. With a patented "Banjo-seat." To prevent *bunching*—

(The door BUZZER sounds again.)

RITA. Would you get that please, Michael—
MIKE. Sure.
(MIKE *goes to door and admits* IRVING LASALLE. IRVING *is an agent—the most elegant agent since Leland Hayward went straight. His striped waistcoat was made for him in Italy. He is particularly proud that the stripes go all the way around.)*
Irving!

(GEORGE rises.)

IRVING. *(Enters)* Michael, dear boy! What a delicious surprise!
RITA. Sneaky! When did you get in?
IRVING. *(To Center)* I flew in this morning. Just for the day. I'm going back on the Ambassador Flight at midnight— My dearest Rita, you look, as always, divine— *(He kisses her hand.)*

(MIKE puts GEORGE'S coat on chair up Left.)

RITA. Sneaky, this is Mr. Kaufman from *PHOTOPLAY*. He's writing a story about me. This is Irving LaSalle. I'm sure you must have heard of him. He's a very famous agent.
GEORGE. How do you do, Mr. LaSalle? *(Puts pencil in Right ear; shakes hands.)*
IRVING. A great pleasure, Mr. MacCauley. A great pleasure, indeed.
RITA. You know, I'm just queer for Sneaky. He's the most intelligent man I know.
(IRVING *crosses up to bar; removes coat.)*

(To GEORGE*)* Why don't you sit down Mr. Kaufman? Over there!
GEORGE. *(Crosses Right; sits on stool)* Thank you.
RITA. Michael is making everybody a vodka martuni before Mr. Kaye gets here. You want one, don't you, Sneaky?—
IRVING. I should adore one, darling! Michael, dear boy, how is your new play progressing?
MIKE. *(Pouring drinks)* Are you kidding? There's no new play— I've started about nine different new plays— but I never get past page three—
IRVING. Well the second play is always the most difficult. I always say that—
MIKE. Look, Irving. I don't want to talk about the second play. I don't want to *hear* about the second play. The hell with the second play. *(Hands drink to* IRVING*)* You know something? I may never write a second play at all. I'm going to the Coast next week to do the screenplay of NO HIDING PLACE—and when it's finished I may never come back— *(He hands martinis to* RITA *and* GEORGE*)*
  (IRVING *sits Right of couch.)*
How's that, baby, okay?
RITA. It's divoon, Michael!
MIKE. *(Up Center)* I may just decide to end my days lying on the golden shores of Malibu, my head cradled in the lap of a sun-kissed starlet, sipping *vin rose* and dictating long, thin movies to fit long, thin screens—
RITA. Michael! Will you please shut up!
  (MIKE *crosses to bar.)*
I mean we only have a few more minutes and poor Mr. Klein here, still hasn't got anything to write about. Have you?
GEORGE. Not too much. No—but this is all very interesting.
RITA. Now where was I? Oh. I know. Why do people misunderstand me? I'll tell you why—they misunderstand me because they don't think of me as a serious actress. You know what they think of me as?

GEORGE. Well—
RITA. *(Sits up)* They think of me as a *sex-symbol.* That's what they think OF ME AS! Do you have any idea at all how many practically undressed pictures of me the studio sends out every week?
GEORGE. No, actually, I don't—
RITA. Do you, Michael?
MICHAEL. No, not actually.
RITA. Twenty-eight to thirty thousand. That's how many—

(MIKE *sits on couch with drink.*)

GEORGE. *(Writing)* Twenty-eight to thirty thousand.
RITA. That's right. Per week. And do you know what they do with them?
GEORGE. Who is that?
RITA. The twenty-eight to thirty thousand people who *get* my practically undressed picture that the studio sends out every week. Do you know what they do with them?
GEORGE. Well, I should imagine—
RITA. They hang them over their beds. *That's* what they do with them. Or sleep with them under their pillows. You know why? So they'll dream about me. That's why! *(Reflectively)* You know something? Half the world is in darkness.
GEORGE. I beg your pardon?
RITA. Half the world is in darkness. I mean it's night time in half the world right now. Oh, you know, in China and places. So that means that there are probably a million different men asleep somewhere dreaming about me right this second! You may not believe this, Mr. Coleman, but I never *wanted* to be a sex symbol. You know what the funniest thing about me is? In person, I'm not really sexy at all. Honest. I'm probably the least sexy person you know! I mean really I am! And I'm just terrible in bed. Everybody says so!
(GEORGE *drops book; puts pencil in ear; picks up book; draws circles; rubs them out.*)
Am I boring you?

(Fortunately, he is saved from replying by the door BUZZER.)

That must be Mr. Kaye. Get it, would you, Michael?

MIKE. Get it, will you Irving?

IRVING. Gladly. *(IRVING goes to the door Left and admits HARRY KAYE.)*

(HARRY is a stereotyped and hackneyed character—a typically stage version of the head of a Hollywood studio. Unfortunately, he is equally typical in real life. Whether, in this case, life has followed art or vice versa is a question too profound to be dealt with here. In any case, HARRY enters.)

IRVING. My dearest Harry!

HARRY. *(Enters. Holds at door)* What the hell are you doing here? This is a private meeting.

IRVING. Dear boy— *(Holds at door.)*

HARRY. *(To Left Center)* Don't "dear boy" me, you shifty-eyed bastard! Let me just tell you—there's nothing here for you to muscle in on. My deal with this Freeman is firm. I bought his play and I already signed him to do the screenplay. So it doesn't make the slightest particle if you represent him or not.

MIKE. Hello, Harry. You want a drink?

HARRY. No. And don't you get plastered before lunch again either. We got to talk business to the broad.

IRVING. Harry—I would like you to meet Mr. George MacCauley. He is interviewing Rita for *MOVIE WORLD*. George—this is Harry Kaye—the head of Rita's studio. *(Back to bar.)*

GEORGE. How do you do, sir?

HARRY. You be sure and get in there how she don't wear no underwear. That's what they want to read about. That's what sells tickets. That's what's made this broad what she is today. No underwear. And don't you forget it.

GEORGE. No, sir. I won't—

HARRY. Okay. *(A step to massage table.)*

RITA. Hello, Harry.

HARRY. Sweetheart. *(He pats her behind)* Putting on a litle weight, ain't ya, kid?
RITA. Just a little, Harry. Right there.
HARRY. Yeah. I can tell.
RITA. Actually it's just these kind of fatty tissues I have— *(To* MASSEUR*)* Isn't that right?
MASSEUR. That's right, Miss Marlowe—
RITA. So all we have to do is break them down—show him how you do it—
 (MASSEUR *works vigorously.)*
Isn't that interesting?

 (IRVING *sits Right arm of couch.)*

HARRY. Yeah, yeah, yeah. But make it snappy. *(Crossing Right via front of massage table)* I got to eat at 12:30 sharp or I start getting these pains—
MASSEUR. I think that's enough for today. Thank you very much, Miss Marlowe.
RITA. I'll go in and get dressed now. You stay here and have another martuni, Mr. McClain and I'll be right back.

 (RITA *in her towel heads Right for the bedroom. The* MASSEUR *rapidly folds up his massage table and exits Left.)*

MIKE. *(Catching him at the door)* You happy in your work?
MASSEUR. *Yes sir! (He exits.)*
MIKE. It figures.
HARRY. *(To* MIKE*)* Is this crook representing you now?
IRVING. I am afraid not, dear Harry. I have been trying for the last six months to persuade young Michael here to become a LaSalle client. But he resists me at every turn. Oh, I'll get him in the end, of course. But as of this moment, alas, I do not represent him.
HARRY. *(Crosses Left. Gives hat and coat to* IRVING

who puts same on chair up Left) He's doing all right. Beat me out of three hundred and fifty grand for that play of his.—I've seen it twice and not one word do I understand. Not one goddamned word.

IRVING. *(At bar)* Michael is one of the few poets writing for the American theatre today— He possesses, according to one New York critic: "An uncanny ear for the lilting speech rhythms of our time."

HARRY. I know. I know. They read me the reviews. *(Crosses to table up Right; deposits ashes)* Look, all I know is the broad talks me into springing three hundred and fifty grand for this guy's play then when I come to find out—what is the story about—the story is about this *hooker* who falls in love with some kind of a *fag!* How we get all this past the Breen Office, I got no idea— *(Two steps Right Center.)*

IRVING. *(To Left Center)* Michael, dear boy, permit me to offer you a friendly word of advice.

MICHAEL. Please do.

IRVING. *(Sits on couch)* Finish your screenplay for Harry as quickly as you can. And then come back to New York and write another play.

MIKE. Irving, I've been giving the matter quite some thought and I have come to the conclusion that I would be out of my mind to write another play.

IRVING. Michael! I am shocked to hear you talk this way. You must realize—you are a very important man. You are perhaps the hottest writer in America today.

MIKE. True, true. You know something? I'm the hottest thing that ever happened. *(Rises; to bar)* Like you say—I'm a very important man. I can get five thousand bucks a week in pictures whenever I want to. *(Puts glass down)* I'm America's number one dinner guest. And dames, Irving, I am betraying no confidence when I tell you that I do very well in that department also.

IRVING. *Really,* Michael!

MIKE. No kidding, Irving. I got it made. I beat the rap, kid. *I beat the rap! (To up Left Center)* I ski in Switzerland—blue shadows on white snow and all that jazz. I park my can on the beach at Antibes. I call Hemmingway *"Poppa"!* I got it *made.* Everything I always wanted. Everything *everybody* always wanted. *(He takes off his shoe and hands it to* IRVING) Here, look at this shoe.

IRVING. I beg your pardon?

MIKE. I would like you to notice this shoe.

IRVING. It appears to be a good, serviceable shoe—

MIKE. This good, serviceable shoe comes from Peal and Company in London. Fifty-six bucks. It is entirely handmade. Manufactured exclusively for me. A very sweet old gentleman in an alpaca coat drew a picture of my foot. Which he now keeps on file together with pictures of feet belonging to Somerset Maugham, Douglas Fairbanks, Jr. and Noel Coward. Look at the goddamn thing. The untutored eye cannot detect it—but there are twenty-seven stitches to the inch in this hunk of footwear. In order for a piece of leather to *withstand* being stitched at twenty-seven times to the inch the hides must be soaked for two years in streams. Mountain streams! *(Takes shoe back and puts it on)* Take the average man. His shoes are held together with spit, for Christ sake. *(Crosses to bar; pours drinks; to Left of couch) Twenty-seven stitches to the inch!* America, Irving, is a wonderful country. A land of opportunity. It is possible to become wildly and insanely successful overnight. One hit play and, as I pointed out, I am suddenly and magically the hottest thing that ever happened. However it works both ways, Irving. It works both ways. One *flop* play and suddenly and magically I am the coldest thing that ever happened. The point is Irving—since NO HIDING PLACE DOWN HERE opened, I have discovered I *like* being a success. *(Crosses up Center, via front of couch)* I *like* making five grand a week in pictures. I *like* taking Rita Marlowe to lunch. I *like* having twenty-seven goddamn stitches to the inch in my shoes. I should write a new play and louse this all up! Am I right Harry?

HARRY. Your second play I don't care about. I only wish you never wrote the *first* one. *(Crosses up Center.)*

RITA. *(At this point* RITA *reappears from the bedroom*

in a cloud of Shalimar wearing a dress of clinging beige jersey) Here we are! That didn't take long, did it? They won't care if I don't wear stockings, will they, Michael? I mean it's just the Pavillion—

MIKE. No stockings, no underwear, Rita I adore you. *(To up Left; picks up coat and puts it on.)*

RITA. *(Two steps to* GEORGE) Now then Mr. Coleman, I just know you're going to write a wonderful story about me, aren't you?

GEORGE. Well, I don't know. I mean it's just—

IRVING. *(Up Right Center)* It is just, my dear Rita, that in your own sweet, child-like way you have not uttered a single word that Mr. MacCauley's magazine could possibly print without gravely jeopardizing its second-class mailing privileges—

HARRY. *(Starting for the door Left)* Look—you just stick to the no underwear and you'll have plenty to write about. C'mon, it's after twelve-thirty and my pains are starting— *(Gives* MIKE RITA's *coat.)*

IRVING. Yes— You cannot keep Harry's pains waiting. But if you like—I have a little time to spare—I should be happy to stay here and regale Mr. MacCauley with printable anecdotes of your rise to fame and fortune—

RITA. Would you really do that, Sneaky? Would that be all right, Mr. Crane?

GEORGE. Well, I guess—if it isn't too much trouble for Mr. LaSalle—

IRVING. Not at all, dear boy. Not at all.

RITA. Thank you, Sneaky. The one thing is, Mr. Cayhill, people who don't know me except from what they read in the papers can't possibly have any idea how unhappy I really am. You know what the whole trouble is? Well, I'll tell you—the whole trouble is my behind!

GEORGE. *(Shocked)* Your—*behind?*

RITA. Yes. It wiggles when I walk—

GEORGE. Well, I wouldn't—

RITA. Sure you would. *(Demonstrating)* **Look. Look at it. Look at it wiggle!** It's not my fault it wiggles. I mean I don't *do* anything. I just walk.

(MIKE *puts coat over her shoulders.*)
You know I think it has something to do with my wearing inexpensive shoes when I was a child.
    (*She is led away by* MIKE *and* HARRY, *still babbling.*)
My feet hurt all the time—

              (They exit.)

    IRVING. *(There is a moment of refreshing silence after their departure)* Well, dear boy, what do you think of our American Goddess of Love?
    GEORGE. I don't know. She makes me want to cry She's so *beautiful!* And so *misunderstood*—
    IRVING. No contest. *(Takes glass from* GEORGE *and crosses to bar)* Now then, if you will allow me to dispose of this sinister concoction. I shall make us a genuine martini—
    GEORGE. Oh, no. No thank you. Not for me.
    IRVING. —ash blonde—stinging cold and altogether divine—
    GEORGE. I seldom, if ever, have one—especially before lunch—and I've already had two—
    IRVING. Dear boy, I insist. If only to remove the taste of this—this *martuni*—
    GEORGE. Look, Mr. LaSalle, this is very kind of you—but you don't really have to stay here and talk to me. And I'm sure you've got so many things to do—you're so busy—
    IRVING. I have nothing to do. Nothing whatsoever. Except to talk to you. It was, in fact, my entire purpose in coming to New York!
    GEORGE. What?
    IRVING. My entire purpose in coming to New York was to talk to you. Please. *(Sits chair Center.)*
    GEORGE. *(Sits)* Talk to me?
    IRVING. *(Up to bar)* Exactly.
    GEORGE. But why? What for?
    IRVING. Supposing I were to tell you that—in some way

—I felt you calling out to me. That I became aware of your—*longings?*

GEORGE. My *longings?*

IRVING. Yes. That strange, ineffable sadness that comes over you when you realize that just beyond a certain secret door there exists another, altogether magic world—inhabited by a chosen few—a world where chauffeur-driven Cadillacs replace subways and bus transfers. A world where all women are beautiful and willing. A world of restaurants and charge accounts—beach houses and little dinners (black tie of course) for Garbo or that new bull fighter or the man who wrote the play. A world created, designed and run exclusively for the happy few who have scaled the heights—who have broken through the sound barrier who have finally—in whatever fashion —achieved—Success. *(Pours drink)* Now, you'd like to be a part of that world, wouldn't you, George?

GEORGE. Yes—sure—I guess so— I mean who wouldn't?

IRVING. Exactly. Who wouldn't? *(Gives* GEORGE *the drink.)*

GEORGE. What is it, Mr. LaSalle? What are you saying?

IRVING. I'm saying the heights can be scaled. The sound barrier can be broken. I've helped many of my clients across that golden threshold. Many, many of them.

GEORGE. I still don't know what you mean?

IRVING. *(To couch; sits on arm)* I shall explain. What I am proposing, quite simply, is that you allow me to represent you—

GEORGE. Represent me?

IRVING. Be your agent. I should be honored to have you for a client.

GEORGE. Mr. LaSalle. This is crazy. I make sixty dollars a week. It just wouldn't be worth your time—

IRVING. *(Rises; crosses back of chair to Right Center)* Let that be my decision, dear boy. I flatter myself not at all when I tell you that in terms of service rendered to my clients—no other literary agent can come close. MCA, the Morris Office—Charlie Feldman—bums—compared to LaSalle—

GEORGE. But I'm not even really a writer. I've really never written anything except this one interview with Rock Hunter. I called it WILL SUCCESS SPOIL ROCK HUNTER? Actually, it was quite well received for what it was. But I'm not really a writer. I have no talent—

IRVING. *Talent?* Dear boy—if talent had anything in the world to do with it—Romanoff's would go out of business— The Ritz bar in Paris would be empty and lower berths on the Ambassador Flight would go begging —we are not speaking of *talent*. We are speaking of *success!* Now, let me repeat—LaSalle service is famous throughout the industry. There is—and—I am speaking quite literally—nothing—but nothing that I cannot do for a client—

GEORGE. You mean you could—like—get me a job at a movie studio—writing a movie?

IRVING. *(Crosses to near couch)* Of course.

GEORGE. But the only thing I've ever written was this one interview. With Rock Hunter. I called it: WILL SUCCESS SPOIL—

IRVING. *(Stops him)* I know. We've been over that before. *(Takes pitcher; pours drink for* GEORGE*)* Here, let me freshen your glass. I fear I have not made myself altogether clear. *There is nothing I cannot do for a client.* Now, let the enormity of that statement sink in. *(Puts pitcher back on bar) There is nothing I cannot do for a client.* For a LaSalle client—his wildest dreams can berome realities. Would you care to win the Nobel Prize for literature— *(Crosses Right)* Run MGM? Know the winner of next year's Kentucky Derby? Speak flawless French without lessons? A client of mine recently became four inches taller. Another, who had been bald as an eagle for years, poor dear, grew a luxurious head of hair. With a suggestion of a wave—right here.

GEORGE. I don't know what you're talking about.

IRVING. *(Left of chair)* Of course you do.

GEORGE. No, I don't.

IRVING. Yes you do.

GEORGE. *(Pauses)* If you were to be my agent—what would you get out of it?

IRVING. My standard arrangement with a new author is as follows: And I may say there is no written agreement. I have nothing in writing with any of my clients. A handshake is sufficient. *(Sits on couch)* Anything you want in the world for ten percent of your soul. *(Takes glass from* GEORGE; *puts it on bar)* Dear boy—you've spilled your martini— As I was saying— Should you, in time to come, require other services of an extraordinary nature—the charge is an additional ten percent for each additional service. *(Pours drink)* I stand ready to back you to the full one hundred percent. *(To* GEORGE *with drink)* Although I assure you—it is rarely if ever necessary.

GEORGE. *(Rises; Right of chair)* This *is* some kind of a joke—

IRVING. As you wish. If, however, it were *not* a joke—would you be interested?

GEORGE. Well, yes—sure— I mean who wouldn't be?

IRVING. Exactly. Who wouldn't be?

GEORGE. *(Takes glass and drinks)* Anything I wanted? Of course I'd be interested. *(Puts glass on table at back)* What do I care about my soul? I don't even believe there is such a thing. You have one life to live and that's all. What use is it to you when you're nobody. Do you think I like living with my aunt in Brooklyn—riding to work in the subways—eating dinner at cafeterias?—I'm twenty-seven years old and I've never had enough money in the bank to take a vacation. *(Crosses down Right Center)* I've never been to bed with a really pretty girl. *(A little bit angry)* Of course I'd be interested. If it wasn't a joke—

IRVING. *(To Left Center)* What would you like?

GEORGE. *(Turns)* What?

IRVING. What would you like?

GEORGE. You can't do this! It's not fair—it's cruel—

IRVING. What would you like?

GEORGE. How do I know? *(To down Left)* Everything. *(Up)* I don't know where to begin. *(Turns)* Yes—I do too. A million dollars. For a start. A million dollars—that's what I'd like.

IRVING. A million dollars?

GEORGE. Sure.

IRVING. If a million dollars is what you really want—it's yours. No contest.

GEORGE. Where is it?

IRVING. Am I to assume that you are now a LaSalle client?

GEORGE. Where is it?

IRVING. First the agreement.

GEORGE. *(Turns front, Left Center)* I'm scared. Suddenly, I'm scared.

IRVING. Dear boy! Of what?

GEORGE. *(To IRVING)* I'm scared it's a joke— *(Away)* And then I'm scared it isn't.

IRVING. *(Tenderly)* Dear boy—

GEORGE. *(Reaches out and shakes IRVING's outstretched hand)* All right. You have a deal.

IRVING. Congratulations. Let's have a drink on this. *(To bar. Mixes drinks)*

(GEORGE *sits on couch.*)

May I tell you it is an honor and a privilege to own ten percent of such a promising—not to say wealthy—young man.

GEORGE. All right. Where's the money?

IRVING. Are you quite sure that a million dollars is really what you want?

GEORGE. That's right.

(IRVING *hesitates for a moment, clearly troubled.*)

What's the matter? You asked me what I wanted and I told you—

IRVING. There is nothing at all the matter. As of this moment there is—at the Irving Trust Company—46th Street branch—a regular checking account in your name —with a balance of one million dollars—less a few pennies for normal service charges and eight dollars and fifty cents for a checkbook with your name imprinted on each check. *(Crosses up Right.)*

GEORGE. *(Rises)* I don't believe you.

IRVING. *(Picks up the phone)* Will you get me the Irving Trust Company, please! 46th Street Branch. 46th at Madison. Thank you— Here you are.

(GEORGE *crosses up and takes phone.*)

Speak to them yourself. *(Crosses down Left)* Ask for the highest ranking official who has not yet gone to luncheon.

GEORGE. *(Taking phone)* I don't know what to say— I feel like a fool— If this is a joke— What should I say—

IRVING. You'll not have to say a great deal—

GEORGE. Hello? This is George MacCauley. Yes— that's right. Of 342 Flatbush Avenue. Yes. I'd like to speak to the highest ranking official who has not yet gone to luncheon. Yes—oh, thank you I'll wait— They're connecting me with the President of the Bank— Hello. Yes, this is Mr. MacCauley speaking. I was calling about my account— What?—It cleared— Oh—a million—yes I certainly will. Thank you, sir— Sure— Sure— Sure— Sure— Yes, I will— Yes, thank you— Yes, I will. Goodbye—

IRVING. *(Takes phone; replaces it; sits on stool Right)* Well, what did he say?

GEORGE. He was really very nice, he thanked me for having such confidence in his bank—he wants to have lunch with me one day real soon—and then show me through the new vault—he was really very nice. Maybe I *will* have another drink now!

IRVING. *(Rises; to bar)* Certainly, dear boy. Certainly.

GEORGE. A million dollars! I'll be damned!

IRVING. *(Pours* GEORGE'S *drink)* You can say that again.

(There is a long pause.)

GEORGE. I guess there's not much point in going ahead with the interview now, is there?

IRVING. I guess not.

GEORGE. I mean there really isn't any reason for me even to go back to the magazine—

IRVING. No—
GEORGE. I mean I'm a millionaire. I can quit my job—
IRVING. That's right.
GEORGE. It would have been a pretty good story, though.
(IRVING *crosses and gives* GEORGE *drink.*)
WILL RITA MARLOWE FIND HAPPINESS AGAIN?
Oh, thank you.
IRVING. Pleasure!
GEORGE. *(Drains martini)* You know, these things are really very tasty.
(IRVING *crosses and sits on couch.*)
I had no idea what I was missing all these years—
IRVING. Most of my clients enjoy martinis at luncheon. And, after all, why shouldn't they? They have very few responsibilities. Everything being—as it is—entirely in my hands—
GEORGE. The thing is, though, now I'll never see her again. *(Wistful)* I mean if I *had* written the story—well—then—at least I could have—you know—called her up or something—after it was published—and asked her how she liked it. This way—of course—well, it's all over. *(Crosses down Right Center)* I'll never see her again.
IRVING. I do believe you are taking an unduly pessimistic attitude. Why can't you see her again—
GEORGE. Well, what would she want to see me for? I mean—she's *Rita Marlowe!* And—even with a million dollars—who am I?
IRVING. *(Rises; to Left Center)* You are a LaSalle client. That's who you are. Do not ever forget it.
GEORGE. I don't know what you mean.
IRVING. Don't you? Well—think about it for a little. Dwell on the implications. Let that wild, free writer's imagination of yours grapple with the problem—think about *her*. Think about *you*. Think about that glorious behind.
GEORGE. I'm thinking.
IRVING. Yes.
GEORGE. You mean you –
IRVING. Eventually, you will get used to the idea that

there is nothing in this world you cannot have. Nothing.

GEORGE. But *Rita Marlowe!*

IRVING. A woman. Like any other woman. Well, not *exactly* like any other woman in a number of ways—I grant you. But still a woman. Capable of loving and being loved. Giving and receiving. Actually, I believe you two would make a very charming couple. *(To couch; sits.)*

GEORGE. *RITA MARLOWE! HOLY COW!*

IRVING. That is an interesting—not to say accurate— way of putting it.

GEORGE. Rita Marlowe— *(Sits chair Right Center.)*

IRVING. My dear boy—you have only to say the word and from this moment forward—until the end of time, if you so desire—Rita will be overcome by a passion for you that would make Isolde's feelings for Tristan seem like Love Finds Andy Hardy.

GEORGE. You mean she'd really like me?

IRVING. *Like you?* She will be able to keep neither her eyes nor her hands off you. Her public displays of affection for you will verge on the embarrassing. And her private displays—*dear boy!*—

GEORGE. *(Rises; Right of chair)* But would it be—you know—*fair?* Wouldn't it be—well, like—taking advantage of her?

IRVING. Rather like that—yes.

GEORGE. I mean it would be a terrible thing to do.

IRVING. Downright shoddy.

GEORGE. I mean—she'd be absolutely helpless.

IRVING. Oh, absolutely.

GEORGE. *(Crosses down Left with drink)* And the awful thing it—she wouldn't be in love with me because she was in love with me—she'd be in love with me because she was—well—*bewitched*—or something.

IRVING. I assure you that—for all practical purposes— you would never notice the difference.

GEORGE. *(Crosses up Left to bar; puts down drink and cigarette)* I couldn't do it. It wouldn't be fair to her. And then there are probably other people involved. I mean she's probably in love with someone else and everything—

IRVING. I do think not. For example—whatever small feelings she may once have held for her husband—from whom she is now separated—have long since passed. I suspect, however, that at this very moment—she feels some small, illicit stirrings for young Michael Freeman—

GEORGE. How can you tell?

IRVING. Dear boy—let me put it this way. Let me say that I have a certain intuition—amounting almost to second sight—in these matters— *(He covers his eyes with his hand, in fierce concentration)* Unless these old eyes deceive me—at this very moment—under the table—Rita and Michael are playing— Forgive me, but I know of no other word to describe it—*footsie*.

GEORGE. Footsie?

IRVING. Yes. Or *toesey-woesey* as it is sometimes called.

GEORGE. I don't understand.

IRVING. *(Pause)* Oh, now really!

GEORGE. *(Kneels Left of* IRVING*)* What? What? What is it?

IRVING. He has taken her foot and placed it on his lap.

GEORGE. How can he do that—right there in the restaurant?

IRVING. Long tablecloth.

GEORGE. Oh. *(Pause. Rises)* Well, you see, that's what I mean. Why shouldn't he? He's got a right to. He's a successful playwright. *(Crosses to Left Center)* He's handsome—he's got everything— You could really make her fall in love with *me*—forever?

IRVING. Dear boy, nothing in this world could be simpler.

GEORGE. Rita Marlowe—in love with me—*me*—forever— *(Softly)* O.K.—if we're going to do it—let's do it—

IRVING. Very well. Dear boy, tell me once again, in your own words—what exactly do you want?

GEORGE. *(Very tensely)* You know what I want. I want Rita Marlowe to love me forever.

IRVING. Very well. So be it. May I tell you that it is an honor to own twenty per-cent of such a promising and wealthy young man who is about to be dragged off to yonder bedroom by the incomparable Rita Marlowe—

(They shake hands. GEORGE's confidence is beginning to ooze a little.)

GEORGE. *(Looks up Right)* My gosh, where is she?

IRVING. Patience. Allow her a moment or two to disengage her foot from the grasp of that grubby playwright. She'll be here soon enough. *(Crosses up Left; takes coat)* Never fear.

GEORGE. Wait, Mr. LaSalle! You can't leave! You got to stay with me—

IRVING. *(Putting on his coat)* Stay with you? Dear *boy!*

GEORGE. *(Steps closer)* Just for a little while. In the beginning.

IRVING. Dear boy, if you need me—and I most sincerely doubt that you will—you have simply to call and I shall fly to your side. *(To door.)*

GEORGE. *(Now genuinely panicked)* Mr. LaSalle I'm *scared!*

IRVING. Dear boy, LaSalle Is Your Shepherd—You Shall Not Want!

(IRVING *exits. A moment later the door opens and* RITA *enters. She is somewhat breathless—a little bewildered and she is wearing only one shoe.)*

RITA. Oh. Hello. You're still here. Oh, I'm so glad. I was afraid you might have gone—

GEORGE. No. I stayed awhile.

RITA. Oh, I'm so glad you did. *(She moves toward him —and he notices that she is wearing only one shoe.)*

GEORGE. What happened to your shoe?

RITA. *(Glancing down and noticing it for the first time herself)* My shoe? Oh. Oh, *that.* I must have taken it off in the restaurant. And left it. I was in such a hurry to leave. I don't know why, exactly. Look, Mr—what is your name anyway—

GEORGE. MacCauley. George MacCauley.

RITA. Well, George— I *can* call you George, can't I?

GEORGE. Sure. Why not? Go ahead. After all, it's my name— *(This dissolves into an idiotic, nervous giggle.)*

RITA. *(Studying him—genuinely puzzled)* I can't understand it at all. You're not a bit bright—or even intelligent, I don't think. As a matter of fact, George, this morning I thought you were an absolute idiot.

GEORGE. You did?

RITA. Let me look at you— *(Pause—while she scrutinizes him from head to toe)* I don't know. I just don't know. God knows you're not handsome—or even very attractive. And yet—George—I can't expect you to understand this—I don't understand it myself—but I— well— *(Crosses to GEORGE) I love you!*

GEORGE. *(Crosses down Left)* Yes. I know.

RITA. *(Following)* You do?

GEORGE. *(Backs Left; then turns up Left)* Yes. Actually, this whole thing is my fault. A serious mistake has been made. On my part of course—

RITA. *(Embraces him)* I love you, darling— *I love you! I love you!*

GEORGE. Oh, no, you don't. You only *think* you do. It's all in your mind—

RITA. All in my *mind?* Oh, *no,* baby!

GEORGE. *(Backs around to up Center)* A very, very serious mistake has been made. I don't know what came over me. I just lost my head, I guess. I'd had this martuni and I'd just gotten this million dollars. And so you see I'm really not responsible. I mean, well, all I can say is it seemed like a good idea at the time. You're so beautiful—so very beautiful and—

RITA. Do you think so, darling? Do you *really* think so?

GEORGE. Oh, yes! Yes I do. And as I was saying to Mr. LaSalle—I'm twenty-seven years old and I've never been to bed with a really pretty girl— *(Backs up, embar-*

rassed) Oh, I'm sorry! Miss Marlowe, forgive me. How could I have said a thing like that—*in mixed company!* It just popped out!

RITA. Is that true, my darling? Is that really true?

GEORGE. That is just popped out, you mean? Oh, yes.

RITA. Do you *swear* it? Do you *swear* you've never been made love to by a beautiful woman—*by a really beautiful woman?* Do you honestly swear it?

GEORGE. Oh, yes. Scout's Honor.

RITA. Oh baby! We're going to be so good for each other! I didn't believe I could feel like this again- - Kiss me, darling—please kiss me—

(She takes him in her arms and kisses him.)

GEORGE. *(Struggling—but she has height and reach on him)* Miss Marlowe—Miss Marlowe— I can't let you do this—it isn't fair to you—

RITA. Darling— I want you, darling— I want you so much—

GEORGE. *Actually,* I blame this whole thing on Mr. LaSalle. He talked me into it—

RITA. Kiss me, darling, kiss me—

GEORGE. "Think about it," he said. "Let your imagination run wild," he told me. "Think about you. Think about her. Think of that glorious behind!" So I did— Oh, Miss Marlowe, all I can say is I—

(She stops him with an enormous kiss. When it is over he finishes his sentence.)

—*told* him I didn't think it was fair to you—and of course it isn't actually—and it isn't at all like me— I've tried, all my life, to be a perfect gentleman—as far as women are concerned— I was brought up—by my aunt, actually—Mother died when I was very young—to have respect for women—

(She kisses him again.)

I don't know what my aunt would say if she could see me now!

RITA. You wait right here— I'll be back in a minute!

Oh baby! Am I ever just queer for you! *(She disappears through the bedroom door, leaving door open.)*

GEORGE. *(Crosses down Right Center. Terrified)* Irving!

(Instantly the door Left opens and IRVING *appears.)*
Oh Mr. LaSalle you got to get me out of this!

IRVING. Out of it? *(Crosses to Center)* Dear boy, do you realize that you are about to fulfill the dream of every red-blooded American male above the age of six— you are about to act out—in reality—the fantasy of an entire nation— I took the liberty of eavesdropping outside the door. I thought you were doing very nicely.

GEORGE. *(Up Center a step)* I can't go through with it. I just can't.

IRVING. *(Crosses Right)* Dear boy, I'm terribly afraid that you will simply have to adjust to your present situation.

GEORGE. *(Crosses to Left Center)* Mr. LaSalle—I lied to you. Remember I told you I was twenty-seven years old and I'd never been to bed with a really pretty girl—well —that's not true—or it *is* true—but it's only partly true— I'm very *shy!* *(Sits on couch)* And well, there's never really been any girl at all— I think I'm going to faint. *(He collapses onto the couch.)*

IRVING. *(Seating himself in a chair at the head of the couch)* Dear boy—don't panic. Your present fears and anxieties are a common emotional experience. One that modern science has duly noted. There is nothing at all to worry about. Two years with a really competent analyst —one who specializes in these matters—two short years and you simply will not know yourself—

GEORGE. *(Sits up)* Two *years?* She'll be out in two *minutes!*

IRVING. Two years would be a rock bottom minimum. At five visits a week—but by the end of that time you would be a veritable Casanova—

GEORGE. *(Rises; crosses Right)* Oh I can't go through with it— It's just— I can't—

IRVING. *(Rises; puts chair up Center)* Dear boy—there is ,of course, another way—

GEORGE. What way?

IRVING. Analysis is useful in its place—but it is rather an unnecessary waste of time and money—for a LaSalle client—

GEORGE. *(A step Center)* You mean you could—

IRVING. Of course—if you want—

RITA'S VOICE. *(Calling—off)* Darling! I'm almost ready—

(There is a pause.)

GEORGE. I want—

(They shake.)

IRVING. Poet, lover, adventurer! Congratulations! I know you will fully adjust to your present situation.

RITA. *(Appears in the doorway. Door is open. She has changed into a peignoir to end all peignoirs. Her eyes devour GEORGE. She is completely oblivious of IRVING'S presence)* Georgie!

(GEORGE *turns to face her—and as he looks at her, his whole attitude and bearing change. Coolly and deliberately he takes a cigarette and sticks it in his mouth. He lights it—striking the match on his thumb nail. Finally, he speaks with a sexy growl. He is suddenly Bogart in Casablanca.)*

GEORGE. Hi ya, kid—

RITA. Oh Georgie!

IRVING. This is one ten per cent you will never regret as long as you live.

(GEORGE *has swept her off her feet and is carrying her bedroomward as*

THE CURTAIN FALLS QUICKLY

ACT TWO

The curtain rises on a rather sumptuous, sun-drenched Hollywood office. Four weeks have passed and the gray slush of New York City seems very far away indeed.

The office is modern, wood-panelled and expensive-looking. Through a vast window, rear wall Center, we can see acres of sound stages. There is no glass in this window. The panes are suggested by black tape borders. A legend on the outer door up Right tells us that we are in the executive offices of RITA MARLOWE PRODUCTIONS. Enormous photographs of the titular head of the company adorn the walls.

At the moment the office is empty except for a very eager and very red-headed SECRETARY *who is engaged in shining the leaves of a poisonous-green, clearly man-eating plant.*

It is about ten-thirty in the morning.

Presently the SECRETARY'S *labors are interrupted by the telephone. She abandons the plant and dashes Left to answer it.*

SECRETARY. *(Sits)* Rita Marlowe Productions— Office of The Vice-President— No, I'm sorry. Mr. MacCauley hasn't come in yet. No. But I'm sure he'll be here by eleven. There's a big story meeting. Mr. Kaye. Miss Marlowe. Everybody— Yes, Mr. MacCauley is going to tell Mr. Kaye the story—and God knows how long that'll take! Yes. I'll tell him you called. All right. Goodbye—

(During this, MIKE FREEMAN has ambled into the office. He is tanner and more healthy-looking than he was four weeks ago—and his clothes have changed from Madison Avenue to Rodeo Drive.)

MIKE. Hello—
SECRETARY. Good morning—
MIKE. Is this Mr. MacCauley's office?
SECRETARY. Yes.
MIKE. Good. *(Crosses down a few steps.)*
SECRETARY. What was it you wanted to see him about?
MIKE. To be perfectly honest I haven't the slightest desire to see him at all.
SECRETARY. Oh. Was your appointment with Miss Marlowe? Miss Marlowe is over on Stage Nine doing retakes for the Joan of Arc Story. She'll be back here at eleven for the story meeting.
MIKE. I have no appointment with Miss Marlowe either. I called her a few times and left messages. But she never called back. *(Crosses up Left to desk)* You know something, I have a feeling she's avoiding me.
SECRETARY. *(Rises)* I see. Well, look—is there anything *I* can do for you?
MIKE. *(He thinks about this for a second)* I don't know. I haven't given it any thought. There must be *something* you could do for me though. Let's see—what *could* you do? Well—you could fix a basket lunch, get a thermos of cold martinis and drive us out to the beach where we could swim naked and make love on the wet sand.
SECRETARY. *(The truth is finally out)* Oh! You're one of the writers, aren't you?
MIKE. *(Looks for cigarette on desk)* Yeah. I'm one of the writers. How did you know?
SECRETARY. I could tell. You talk like a writer.
MIKE. I do?
SECRETARY. Oh, yes. They always talk about swimming naked and making love on the wet sand—

MIKE. *(Reaches for matches; lights cigarette)* They do?

SECRETARY. Sure. That's practically all they *ever* talk about. Oh, sometimes they talk about their income taxes. But mostly it's the old: "Oh, let's swim naked and make love on the wet sand" routine.

MIKE. That's very interesting. Why do you suppose that is?

SECRETARY. Oh, because writers are mostly—impractical. You know—like—dreamers—

MIKE. Oh, how do you mean exactly?

SECRETARY. Well, anybody with any sense—even a writer—should know you can't make love on *wet sand*. I mean it's all damp and cold and it's impractical—

MIKE. You know something? *(Sits chair Right)* This cult of neo-realism is destroying our whole racket.

SECRETARY. *(To Right Center)* I mean like when I saw FROM HERE TO ETERNITY I just laughed and laughed. That scene on the beach. I sent it to Sidney Skolsky as a "Movie Boner." I said: "Go try it sometime. You'll see. It just can't be done on wet sand." But he didn't print it.

MIKE. Skolsky was chicken.

SECRETARY. I guess so. What kind of a writer are you? I'm always interested in the different kinds.

MIKE. I am a playwrote.

SECRETARY. A what?

MIKE. *A PLAYWROTE.* That's a playwright who hasn't written anything *lately*—

SECRETARY. *(To couch)* I think that's just fascinating. Are you a friend of Mr. MacCauley's?

MIKE. In a way, yes. In a way.

SECRETARY. Mr. MacCauley is such an interesting man. He doesn't say very much but you can see how *deep* he is. Miss Marlowe found him in New York, you know.

MIKE. *SO* I heard. Yes.

SECRETARY. Now he's Vice President—and he's writing her new picture. She wouldn't make a move without him.

MIKE. Well, that's America for you. In a democracy—

(GEORGE MACCAULEY *enters outer office, leaving door open. His costume is even more Hollywood than* MIKE'S, *or maybe it's just that he should never be permitted to wear Italian sport shirts in public. He begins rummaging around on* SECRETARY'S *desk down Right.*)

GEORGE. *(Calling)* Miss Logan, do we have any aspirin?

SECRETARY. Mr. MacCauley!

GEORGE. *(To Right Center)* Miss Logan—I don't know why we're out of aspirin. I thought we ordered the *family* size.

MIKE. Well—hail the conquering hero.

GEORGE. Oh hello, hello Mr. Freeman.

MIKE. Hi ya George.

GEORGE. Mr. Freeman—it's good to see you again— come in. Oh, you are in.

SECRETARY. *(Comes up with glass of water and two aspirin)* Mr. MacCauley! Aspirinsville!

(As he takes the glass and two aspirin.)

Fire one! Fire two!

GEORGE. Thank you, Miss Logan. That will be all for now.

SECRETARY. *(Crosses Right)* All right, Mr. Mac-Cauley. *(Stops; turns)* Now, whenever you're ready to start dictating, you just buzz me.

GEORGE. I will. I will. I'll certainly do that. I'll buzz you.

SECRETARY. All right?

GEORGE. All right.

(SECRETARY *exits to outer office.*)

Miss Logan—she's very eager—

MIKE. Eager! Yes, I know what you mean.

GEORGE. *(Sits on couch)* It's funny, but somehow I get the feeling that she's disappointed in me. She keeps expecting me to dictate something to her. I've been out here for four weeks now and I still haven't been able to think of anything to dictate.

MIKE. Hey, George, I got a message I was supposed to report here. Any idea what it's about?

GEORGE. Here? No. They didn't tell me anything about it. Look, Mr. Freeman. I've been wanting to tell you. I'm awful sorry about what happened. I mean about the movie. You were all set to write it—and then Rita changed her mind. Actually it was all my fault—and I feel just terrible about it. Just terrible.

MIKE. In what way?

GEORGE. Well, how you must feel—

MIKE. Oh, I feel like one of the idle rich—a very pleasant sensation.

GEORGE. Oh, you must have had a contract?

MIKE. That's right.

GEORGE. So they had to pay you anyway—

MIKE. Yeah. It's sort of like clipping coupons. *(Rises; to Left Center)* Have you ever stopped to think how much money it would take invested in two percent tax-exempt bonds to produce an unearned income of five thousand dollars a week?

GEORGE. No, actually, I haven't.

MIKE. I have. I figured it out in my spare time. Thirteen million dollars.

GEORGE. My gosh. *(Rises)* Do they send it to you or do you have to come and pick it up?

MIKE. Oh, I guess they'd send it to me if I asked them. But I like to come by and pick it up. It kind of gives me a connection with reality. Actually it was a big mistake. I should of had them send it to me. This morning when I stopped by to pick up this week's five thousand dollars, they suddenly told me they wanted me to report to your office.

GEORGE. To my office? Isn't that interesting!

MIKE. Interesting? *(Crushes cigarette)* It's a goddamn imposition. I was on my way to the tennis club— Charlie Lederer and I got a thousand dollar bet we can beat Segura and Herbie Flam—the only thing is they have to play handcuffed together.

(GEORGE *sits again.*)

No kidding, it's going to be the sporting event of the year. Actually, I feel sorry for *you*— I don't know how the hell you're going to beat the story for pictures. The prostitution thing is rough enough but then you still have the homosexual angle. *(Sits Right of* GEORGE) Listen, if you don't mind talking about it, I'd love to hear what you've got in mind. I *do* have kind of a rooting interest in the thing. What's the matter? You look like you're going to cry—

GEORGE. *(Rises)* Look, Mr. Freeman—if I tell you something—can it be in confidence? *(Crosses up Left to desk.)*

MIKE. Sure—and will you please for God sake call me Mike—

GEORGE. All right. Thank you. That's very nice of you, Mike. And I'm certainly glad you're taking it this way. I mean you can't believe how everybody resents me. That's why it's so nice that you feel the way you do. I mean I just don't feel *wanted* at all. *(Sits on couch)* Mr. Kaye, for instance, Harry, he absolutely hates me. When Rita told him I was going to write the movie—it was just awful—first he yelled and screamed and then he cried. He's a very emotional man.

MIKE. *(Rises)* So I've heard, yeah. *(To down Right; sits.)*

GEORGE. It was just awful. It was at lunch. He just sat there and cried. It was really amazing— I've never seen anybody before who could cry and eat at the same time. *(Rises; crosses down Right Center)* And if you think Mr. Kaye hates me, you should see Mr. Brannigan. He's Rita's ex-husband. Well not really her ex-husband—they're only separated—he won't give her a divorce. Anyway, he's threatened to kill me. He plays left tackle for the Los Angeles Rams.

MIKE. Jealous, is he?

GEORGE. Oh, very jealous. See—he used to be vice-president. But we voted him out of office. Listen, Mike, what time is it?

MIKE. It must be about quarter of eleven.

GEORGE. My gosh— *(Crosses Left to desk.)*
MIKE. What's the matter?
GEORGE. Well there's this big conference with Mr. Kaye, Rita, and everybody at eleven—and I'm supposed to tell them what I'm going to do to the play so they can do it as a movie. That's probably why they wanted you here—they probably want to have you listen to it too.
MIKE. Yeah. That's probably it. Look—why don't you just tell it to me now—then I could beat it.
GEORGE. The thing it Mike, I don't have anything to tell them. Not anything at all. *(He buzzes for* SECRETARY.*)*
SECRETARY. *(Bursts in; quickly to desk)* Yes, Mr. MacCauley. Were you ready to start dictating?
GEORGE. No. No. Not yet. I just want you to try to get hold of Irving LaSalle. It's very important. They'll be here any minute.
SECRETARY. All right, Mr. MacCauley. Now whenever you're ready to start dictating—you buzz me.
GEORGE. I will. I certainly will. I'll do that. I'll buzz you—
SECRETARY. You do that.
GEORGE. I will.

(She finally leaves, closing door up Right; sits at her desk.)

MIKE. She's not eager, she's ready.
GEORGE. *(Sits at desk. To* MIKE*)* You see I've never written a movie before. I just have no idea how it's done. I was going to take an extension course in screenplay writ'ng at UCLA—you know—nights. But Rita wouldn't let me. She said it wouldn't look good—and besides she likes me to get to bed early. But I suppose it's only natural—I imagine the first thing you write is always the hardest.
MIKE. *(To front of couch)* I don't like to discourage you or anything. But the first one is a cinch. It's the second one that's murder. I wrote my play in six weeks. It

was a breeze. But that was two years ago and I haven't written a line since. From the minute Brooks Atkinson said I was a young Thornton Wilder I was a dead pigeon. Now, everytime I write a goddamn line I look at it and say—would a young Thornton Wilder write a line like that? And the answer is always no. So I tear it up. That's why I told them I'd do the movie. I figured *anybody* can write a movie. The big trick is to sit *through* one.

GEORGE. I can't. I mean I can't write one. As a matter of fact the only thing I ever wrote in my life was an interview with Rock Hunter. I called it: WILL SUCCESS SPOIL ROCK HUNTER? Actually, it was quite well received for what it was. The magazine got a number of letters about it—

(This dreary recital is cut off by the arrival of IRVING LASALLE *through up Right door.)*

SECRETARY. *(Ushering him in)* Mr. LaSalle!
IRVING. *(To Right of* MIKE*)* Dear boy.
GEORGE. *(Rises. To down Left)* Irving!
IRVING. And *Michael!* What a pleasant surprise!
GEORGE. *(Desperately)* Irving, it's almost eleven o'clock—
IRVING. Dear boy, do I detect a note of panic in your voice?
GEORGE. The story meeting! It's going to start in a couple of minutes!
IRVING. *(Glancing at his watch)* Seven minutes—to be exact. Dear boy, what is your problem?
GEORGE. *(Crosses down Right)* Well, the thing is, they're paying me all this money to write a movie—so naturally they expect me to—you know—*write something.*
IRVING. That is the cross every writer must bear. The necessity of at least occasionally writing something is the one hideously jarring note in what is otherwise an almost ideal way of life. Am I right, Michael?
MIKE. Don't ask me. I haven't written a line in two

years— *(He has taken a handful of stationery from the desk. To* GEORGE*)* Hey, George, you mind if I take some of this? My mother thinks I work here—

GEORGE. Help yourself—

MIKE. Thanks.

GEORGE. Irving, you know I can't write a movie. I can't write anything—

IRVING. *(Sits on couch)* I grant you that Michael's play —brilliant as it is—does present some unusual problems for the screen. Prostitution has, as you know, recently become acceptable to the Breen office—if handled with the utmost delicacy and good taste. And if the young lady in question also dies an especially harrowing and violent death at the end. Homosexuality, however—even implied homosexuality—is another matter. You will have to summon all your ingenuity.

GEORGE. Irving I don't have any ingenuity! I don't even know how to *begin* to write a movie!

IRVING. The *beginning* of a movie is childishly simple. The boys and the girl meet. The only important thing to remember is that—in a movie—the boy and the girl must meet in some *cute* way. They cannot, you understand, just be introduced. Or meet like normal people at, perhaps, a cocktail party or some other social function. No. It is terribly important that they meet cute.

MIKE. You can write that down if you want to—

(He notices that GEORGE *is.)*

Oh you *are*.

GEORGE. "Meet cute"?—I don't understand, Irving—

IRVING. For example—the boy enters a department store to purchase a pair of pajamas. He wears only pajama *bottoms*—he does not wish to buy a whole pair. He wishes to purchase only the bottoms. The store will not sell him just the bottoms. Nearby is a beautiful girl who is *also* seeking to buy pajamas. But only the tops. The solution is obvious. Our boy and our girl—strangers until this moment—suddenly find themselves the joint owners of a single pair of pajamas. *(Crosses Right)* In short they have met cute. *(Crosses to couch; sits.)*

GEORGE. *(Rises; crosses Center)* I think that's just remarkable. Maybe I could have Rita buying pajamas. Of course she doesn't wear pajamas in real life. As a matter of fact, actually, she doesn't wear anything at all in bed.

MIKE. That statement—is it fact or hearsay?

GEORGE. Oh, it's a fact—

MIKE. *(Studies* GEORGE *carefully and with some awe. Shaking his head)* Amazing! Only in a democracy— I tell you—

GEORGE. Huh? Well anyway— I was figuring—maybe I could have Rita go into the store and—

IRVING. Dear boy, I beg of you—forget the pajamas. *(Reclines on couch)* The pajamas has been done. It was simply an illustration. But now that you have grasped the technique, you can make up a perfectly charming one of your own. The boy in Michael's play, you remember, is a psychiatrist.

(GEORGE *sits Right.*)

The girl is a prostitute. I can imagine infinite possibilities. Dear Michael. How did they meet in your play?

MIKE. She just comes to his office. It's a one set show.

GEORGE. That's pretty good. Maybe she just comes to his office—

IRVING. No, no, no, no! You are missing the whole point. They must meet cute. *(Scornfully) Comes to the office,* really—

GEORGE. Irving, you've got to help me figure out something.

(There is a long pause.)

MIKE. *(Dreamily)* I'll bet you *two hundred dollars* it can be done on wet sand!

GEORGE. What?

MIKE. *(Rises)* Look, you don't have anything like a bottle of whiskey around here do you?

GEORGE. No—

MIKE. I just thought I'd ask—

(At this moment RITA appears in the outer office. She has come directly from Stage Nine and her retakes. She is still in full costume for her role. It is apparently the studio's opinion that The Maid of Orleans went into battle wearing a skin-tight, gold lame leotard. However, on RITA is looks very good.)

SECRETARY. Good morning, Miss Marlowe!
IRVING. The divine Rita!
RITA. Sneaky! When did you get in?
IRVING. *(Rises; Left of her)* This morning. Let me look at you— *(He holds her at arm's length.)* Gentlemen, this is not an actress *playing* Joan of Arc. This *is* Joan of Arc. No contest.
RITA. *(Brandishing her sword and striking an heroic pose)* "If a truce is signed with Burgundy I shall never wear this armor again! I told my people to ride boldly among the enemy, and I, myself, rode boldly among them!"

(There is a brief, nervous silence after this which is finally broken by MIKE.)

MIKE. Motion pictures are your best form of entertainment.
RITA. *(Coming back to earth—and turning to IRVING)* Unscrew me, will you, Sneaky.
  (IRVING assists in the removal of a piece of her armor; sets it up back. At this point she notices MICHAEL.)
Oh, Michael! How are you?
MIKE. Divoon, darling. Just divoon, thank you.
GEORGE. Hey kid—I thought I told you not to come shaking your butt around this office while I'm working— the story meeting's not for another five minutes yet—
RITA. I know, doll baby. But we got finished early— and I had to talk to you. It's something important. You do forgive me, just this tiny once—don't you, Georgie?
GEORGE. Sure kid. Put 'er there!

(They fall into a passionate embrace.)

MIKE. *(Watches this. He is awed all over again. He shakes his head and mutters. Crossing down Right)* I don't understand it—stone me—but I don't understand it—

IRVING. *(To* MIKE*)* As I keep telling you, dear boy. All you need is a good agent.

GEORGE. Now then, kid. What seems to be the trouble?

RITA. Georgie, it's Bronk. He's started up again. He must have read about us in the papers or something. He called this morning right after you left. He sounded terribly mad and he kept threatening the most awful things—

MIKE. You are speaking, I presume, of the so very athletic Mr. Brannigan?

RITA. Yes. He's such a wild one. I'm scared of him. Really I am. You won't believe this, but that boy is still absolutely queer for me. There's nothing he can do about it while he's in training, of course— *(Crosses Left to desk)* But the minute the football season is over he kind of flips his lid. I mean he's got all that energy—and it has to go *someplace—*

GEORGE. Baby, I wouldn't worry about him. What can he possibly do to you?

RITA. *(Crosses to couch)* Well, he didn't mention doing anything to *me.* Except the usual, of course—

(Pause.)

MIKE. Oh. *That* old thing—

RITA. Yes. But he mostly kept talking about what he was going to do to poor Georgie—

GEORGE. Oh. Oh, I see— *(Sits at desk.)*

(There is a pause.)

MIKE. *(Dreamily)* What would you say old Bronk *weighs* these days?

RITA. Well, the last time I saw him he weighed 230. That was stripped of course.

MIKE. Yeah—

RITA. *(Brightly)* He weighs even more with his clothes on.

MIKE. It figures—

GEORGE. *(With ringing lack of conviction)* These big men—all muscle-bound. Can't fight their way out of a paper bag. Why I was reading just the other day—the small, wiry chap can take the bigger fellow everytime—

MIKE. I never noticed—are you an especially *wiry* chap, Georgie?

(Outside: the SECRETARY's *PHONE rings. She answers it, then quickly buzzes* GEORGE.*)*

SECRETARY. Excuse me, Mr. MacCauley. But Mr. Kaye's office just called. It's eleven o'clock and Mr. Kaye is on his way down. *(Hangs up.)*

RITA. What is it, Georgie?

GEORGE. It's eleven o'clock and Mr. Kaye is on his way down.

RITA. Goody! *(Sits atop couch.)*

GEORGE. *(Looks desperately at* IRVING *and crosses Right)* That thing we were talking about—that *I* was telling *you*- about—you know—with the pajamas—you're sure it's been done?

IRVING. Absolutely. By Billy Wilder. In BLUEBEARD'S EIGHTH WIFE with Gary Cooper and Claudette Colbert. *(Crosses Left.)*

RITA. *(Sits Right arm of couch)* I'm so excited. I can hardly wait. You won't believe this, Sneaky—but Georgie hasn't told me a single word about the story—not a single word— I can hardly wait.

(Close shot: GEORGE's *stricken face.)*

GEORGE. Irving—

IRVING. *(The United States Marines)* Dear boy— I know how eager you are to spring this little yarn of yours on Harry—but I most strongly urge you not to divulge a word—not a single word—until your new concept has jelled just a bit more firmly—

GEORGE. What? That's just what I was thinking—jelled—

RITA. Now Sneaky, if Harry wants Georgie to tell him the story—Georgie is just going to have to tell him. You know how Harry is—

IRVING. *(Crosses Right Center)* Yes. I know how Harry is. I must insist—eager as you are to speak—that you permit me—as your agent—to do the talking-- I have been telling stories to Harry for years—and I have discovered that when you have nothing to tell him—it is sometimes possible to *distract* him— Let me handle everything— Rita—on the couch please. Michael, up there beside Rita. And George, in order to give the illusion of great industry, perhaps it would be better if you were over there—at the typewriter.

(GEORGE *goes to desk Left and seats himself at the typewriter.*)

Typing something!

GEORGE. What should I type?

IRVING. How should I know! Have you written a long, chatty letter to your aunt lately?

(GEORGE *begins to type furiously. Or as furiously as you can type with one finger.* IRVING *surveys the scene— he is pleased with it.* HARRY *is ushered into the office.*)

IRVING. My dearest Harry—

HARRY. Never mind "my dearest Harry"! What's the story?

RITA. Hello, Harry—

MIKE. Hi Harry— Remember me?

HARRY. Remember you? I'd like to forget you. Five thousand dollars a week. The highest paid tennis player in America.

(Indicating GEORGE—*who is typing.)*
I only hope *he's* got something that's all.

IRVING. Look at him. Such powers of concentration—completely oblivious of his surroundings—lost in a dream world of his own making— *(Calling to* GEORGE) Dear boy —Mr. Kaye is here!

(GEORGE *rises; crosses Center.)*

HARRY. Four weeks I been waiting and still I didn't see a page. Not a single page—

IRVING. Art, my dear Harry, is long. And time is fleeting—

HARRY. Don't tell me art. For thirty-two years in this industry I had every great writer working for me. Aldous Huxley. Maxwell Anderson. Edgar Rice Burroughs. And from every one of them—ten pages a week—like clockwork— *(Crosses up Left Center.)*

GEORGE. *(Crossing nervously to* HARRY) How do you do, sir?

HARRY. Never mind how do you do. What's the story? *(He walks briskly to the desk and sits.)*

IRVING. Harry, the boy is making progress. Great progress. For the first time he knows where he is going. He has a new direction.

HARRY. Has he got a new story—with no hookers and no fags?

IRVING. This boy is going to make you a movie you'll be proud of. Something with stature. This is going to be an important motion picture.

(HARRY *suddenly notices the sheet of paper in the typewriter; fascinated, he rips it out and reads what* GEORGE *has written.)*

HARRY. *(Reading)* My, "Dear Aunt Jessie"—? Uh, huh, here's a switch! The hooker is now somebody's aunt!

IRVING. *(Quickly—to the rescue)* Aunt Jessie is just a minor character. A wonderful bit, however. Warm, human—but with a ready wit and a dry humor. Georgie here was hoping you could get Ethel Barrymore.

HARRY. Okay. Okay. Never mind Ethel Barrymore. Just tell me the story—

IRVING. Harry. I'm going to give it to you in shorthand. I'll give it to you in just one word. This boy has written about—*people!*

HARRY. *(Exploding) What people!*

IRVING. *(Topping him)* A prostitute and a psychiatrist! It's a story—dear Harry—that could have been done in no other time and in no other place. It is a story of today—now—a story that combines a worthwhile spiritual message with a strong sex angle. *(Crosses Right Center)* Picture if you will, a world gone mad—sipping vodka martinis and dancing the mambo in the very shadow of the H Bomb—

HARRY. Please. Please. I am an old man. A naturalized citizen. All these modern things—vodka cocktails the mambo I don't know about. Just tell me, so I can understand it—what is the story?

IRVING. It's a story, my dearest Harry, that is everybody's story. But the great thing. The wonderful thing. *(Crosses to desk)* The magic thing—is that every man woman and child who sees this picture is going to know that *you* did it. It's going to be your kind of picture. It's going to have your personal stamp on it. And, next April, when this boy here is standing up there on the stage of the Pantages Theater—and they hand him the Academy Award— *(He takes water jug from the desk and hands it to* GEORGE *with great ceremony)* You know what he is going to do? He's going to turn to that vast audience—and he's going to say—"Ladies and gentlemen of the motion picture industry, I thank you. I thank you from the bottom of a heart that is, at this moment, almost too full to speak. But"—he's going to say—"this simple golden statuette—this symbol of everything that is good and fine and wholesome in this great industry of ours—belongs not to me—but to another man—that man whose courage, and vision, and taste is so clearly stamped

on every single foot of this film." And then he's going to turn and he's going to call you up out of that audience—
(HARRY *rises, spellbound; to front of desk.*)
And there—before the television cameras—he is going to hand his Oscar to you— *(He takes the water jug from* GEORGE *who has been holding it rather foolishly and presents it to* HARRY) And he's going to say—very simply—but with all his heart— "Harry—take it. It belongs to you." *(Crosses Right Center, back to audience.)*

HARRY. *(Caught, for a moment, in the spell of* IRVING's *oratory,* HARRY *holds the jug proudly in his hands and steps forward to make a speech)* I am touched. *(Crosses Left Center, front)* As many of you may know I came to this country—an immigrant boy—in the year 1902— I had fourteen dollars and a pair of gold-rimmed spectacles. *(Giving way to emotion, he blurts out:)* America has been good to me! *(He goes on—the tears streaming down his face)* My friends, for forty-three years in this industry which I have helped to build—I have tried to make fine pictures that would also do good at the box-office. I have, in this time, made many great pictures that I am proud of. But I have always said—most humbly—that no matter how much you pay for a property—no matter what great stars you put in it—a motion picture is—first—last—and always—the creation of the man who first sat down in a lonely room and put the story on paper. The Writer! My boy—and if—God willing—I had a son—he should only be like you—you wrote this story—you earned this—take it—it's yours! *(He hands the water jug back to the glassy-eyed* GEORGE) All I ask in return is—*what the hell is the goddamn story about?*

(HARRY *turns up Left; sits at desk.* GEORGE *stands holding the jug.* IRVING *has done all an agent can do. The situation is out of hand. Gamely, however, he tries once more.)*

IRVING. Harry, this boy has written the greatest—

HARRY. *(Bellowing) He* won the Academy Award! Let *him* tell it!

RITA. Yes, darling. Don't pay any attention to Irving. Go right ahead and tell us the story—

GEORGE. *(Gulps helplessly)* Well—

(There is a long, horrible, sickening, deathly pause. IRVING coolly lights a fresh cigar. Then he looks at GEORGE. He watches him for a moment, then clears his throat. GEORGE looks over at IRVING, nods frantically. IRVING shrugs an "okay-the-client-is-always-right" shrug.)

Maybe I better tell them the story, Irving.

(He looks at HARRY who is watching him, stony-faced. He looks at RITA who smiles meltingly.)

RITA. Please do, Georgie. For me—

(He thinks a moment longer—begins surreptitiously to count on his fingers.)

IRVING. *(Helpfully)* Forty—

GEORGE. Okay.

IRVING. Dear boy, are you absolutely sure?

GEORGE. Yes. I just want to tell them the story.

IRVING. So you shall, dear boy, and so you shall. But, first permit me, however, to say that it is a pleasure to have forty percent of a young man who, in addition to all of his other virtues, has been able to lick NO HIDING PLACE DOWN HERE for pictures.

HARRY. Come on, my boy, speak up, speak up!

GEORGE. *(Stands waiting—a blank expression on his face. Then it happens. And when it does his whole manner changes. He becomes authoritative and sure)* As you all know, the first and most difficult problem in the construction of a motion picture is to contrive what we in the trade call a "meet cute" for the boy and girl. And I do believe that I have succeeded in coming up with rather an ingenious one. The boy is a psychiatrist. The girl is a prostitute. All right. How do they meet?

HARRY. *(Fascinated)* Okay, how *do* they meet?

MIKE. She come to his office?

GEORGE. *(Scornfully) Comes to his office! Dear boy!* Each of them has sent his couch out to be recovered! *(Crosses to desk)* But there is a mix-up—and *her* couch is delivered to his office—and *his* couch is delivered to her apartment. He goes to her apartment to get his couch back. "I need it for my work!" he says. And she says: "I need it for my work!"

*(There is pandemonium and triumph—*HARRY *is embracing* GEORGE *as*

THE CURTAIN FALLS

ACT THREE

Scene I

SCENE: *The office.*

A year has passed. It is night in late March. The toilers have left the vineyards. The great studio is empty, except for one toiler, the SECRETARY.

At rise she is busy adjusting antennae of portable television set on the desk up Left. It is arranged to face the couch upstage Left Center. She turns it on. While it is warming up she scurries to her desk—gets small picnic basket, brings it to the couch. Turns TV up slightly, settles down on couch, takes sandwich from basket and settles back to watch. From the TV set comes the sound of what will shortly prove to be the ACADEMY AWARDS — TAPE RECORDING AUDIO CUE HERE—

MIKE FREEMAN *appears in the up Right doorway. He carries a handsome Mark Cross dispatch case—* "And now to read the names of the five nominees for achievement in SOUND RECORDING here is RICARDO CORTEZ."

MIKE. Hello. Anybody home?
SECRETARY. *(Jumping up)* Why, Mr. Freeman! Long time no see!
MIKE. You know, I wish you hadn't said that.
SECRETARY. Said what?
MIKE. "Long time, no see." It's just that—have you

ever noticed that girls who say "long time no see" also like Chinese food?
(She regards him blankly.)
The whole thing is totally irrelevant. I'm sorry I brought it up— Am I interrupting something?

SECRETARY. Of course not. I was just watching the Academy Awards.

MIKE. Oh, well, just so it isn't anything *important*.

(He walks over and casually switches off the set. Kill TV SOUND here. He does this—not rudely—but automatically. He is clearly a man who goes around switching off TV sets. For which we can only love him.)

SECRETARY. What are you doing here anyway? I mean why aren't *you* at the Awards?

MIKE. Because I am not a masochist. *(Notices that she is eating)* That isn't egg roll, is it?

SECRETARY. No.

MIKE. *(Briefcase to couch)* I'm glad. As a matter of fact I was taking a walk—then I saw your light.

SECRETARY. A walk?

MIKE. *(Through speech he opens briefcase—takes out bottle of Scotch—glasses—makes drinks, gives one to her. Knee on couch; looks out window)* That's right. I come over here almost every night, for a walk. It's the damndest thing. Over there on the back lot they got an exact replica of Fifth Avenue—from 57th Street to Radio City. It's just great—of course you can't get a cab or anything—but then you can't get a cab on Fifth Avenue either—it's really a technical masterpiece—every detail is perfect—they even have pigeon droppings on the sidewalk in front of St. Pat's—talk about special *effects!*—only instead of Saks Fifth Avenue—whatta they got—a bunch of goddamn palm trees.

SECRETARY. You know, there is one thing I can never understand about the writers. If they all hate it so much out here—*why don't they go back* where they came from?

MIKE. Because, Miss Logan, back there is Reality. Snow, elevator men, producers clamoring for your unwritten second play. Here—we sit in the glorious sunshine dreaming dreams of collapsible independent companies, set up for capital gains stirring only to present each other with golden statues for achievement in set dressing—black and white. *(He snaps the TV set back on.)*

SECRETARY. Honest to God, in many ways you're even *deeper* than Mr. MacCauley!

(MIKE, *wordless, pours another drink. As the TV set comes back on we now hear a female voice.)*

VOICE. The nominees for the Best Screenplay of the year! Here they are! Billy Wilder. Leonard Spiegelgass. Richard Brooks. Daniel Taradash. Milton Sperling.

(There is applause and other appropriate noises. Through this the conversation continues. MIKE *sits on couch.)*

SECRETARY. Mr. MacCauley wasn't even nominated! It was an outrage! Did you see the picture?
MIKE. Part of it—
VOICE. Envelope please—thank you!
SECRETARY. I can hardly wait—
MIKE. The suspense is killing me—or *something* is—
VOICE. *(High drama)* Wait a minute—ladies and gentlemen—wait a minute—something extraordinary has happened—wait a minute— *(Portentiously)* I think we are about to witness *history in the making!*

(Fade SOUND out.)

SECRETARY. What is it?
MIKE. Adolph Hitler has been found alive—he's running a delicatessen in Minneapolis—

(Up SOUND.)

VOICE. It's an upset— An upset— By an overwhelming last minute, write-in vote—the winner of the Best Screenplay is George MacCauley—for "NO HIDING PLACE DOWN HERE!"

(This causes a riot at Pantages. The SECRETARY *is squealing with delight.)*

MIKE. My God—
SECRETARY. Look— Look—there's Mr. MacCauley—with Miss Marlowe— And isn't that Mr. LaSalle—shaking his hand?
MIKE. Good old reliable Irving—
SECRETARY. There he goes up onto the stage—doesn't he look just beautiful!
MIKE. Yeah—that crewcut though—under the lights—the scalp kind of shines through—

(There is APPLAUSE and CHEERS. The SECRETARY *bursts into tears of joy. She clutches* MIKE, *who comforts her; at the same time reaches back and turns off set. Kill SOUND.)*

SECRETARY. This is the happiest day of my life— *(Picks up basket, places it on shelf at back.)*
MIKE. Why?
SECRETARY. I never worked for a writer who won an Oscar before— *(Her hanky is out, blowing nose and trying to pull herself together)* I once had a writer—his picture was such a big hit that they named a sandwich after him at the Commissary—it was just tuna fish salad on French toast but I cried anyway so you can just imagine how I feel now—
MIKE. *(Pouring drink)* I must say I'm a little shaken myself— *(Clinch.)*

(At this moment the door to the office opens and BRONK *enters.)*

ACT III WILL SUCCESS SPOIL ROCK HUNTER? 55

BRONK. *(His manner is exaggeratedly polite—which only serves to underline the menace)* Rita Marlowe Productions?

SECRETARY. *(Pulling herself together. Breaks embrace)* That's right.

BRONK. Office of the Vice-President?

SECRETARY. Yes.

BRONK. Is the Vice-President *here?*

SECRETARY. *(Right Center)* Of course not. The Vice-President just won the Academy Award.

BRONK. I know. I was watching it. In a restaurant across the street. *(Casually he walks to the bookcase up Right Center, reaches behind the books and takes out an exerciser which he begins to use.)*

SECRETARY. Who shall I say called?

BRONK. Let's say, a *Past* Vice-President— I *thought* I left this thing here—

SECRETARY. You're Bronko Brannigan!

BRONK. *(To down Right Center. Still exercising)* Uh-huh.

MIKE. Not *the* Bronko Brannigan? Who weighs 230 stripped. And even more with his clothes on?

BRONKO. Something like that—yeah— Course when I'm in training I shade it a couple of pounds.

MIKE. *(Coming up)* Name of Freeman. *(Crosses down.)*

BRONK. *(Stops exercising and extends his hand)* Pleasure. *(He tosses the exerciser to the couch, then ambles to the desk and removes TV set and other breakables.)*

SECRETARY. What are you doing?

BRONK. I wouldn't want it to become damaged—in the *scuffle.*

MIKE. *(Has picked up exerciser, tries it without success)* You do this frequently?

BRONK. Yeah. I skip rope a lot too.

MIKE. *(Tosses exerciser to ledge up Right)* Uh-huh. *(Picks up his bottle)* I don't suppose you indulge?

BRONK. Never touch it.

MIKE. You don't mind if I do?

BRONK. Not at all.

SECRETARY. *(To Left behind* BRONK*)* Was there anything special you wanted with Mr. MacCauley—or is this a social call?

(BRONK *takes the phone wire, wraps it around his fist and snaps it. Crosses Right, snaps telephone wire on* SECRETARY's *desk too.)*

BRONK. Just social.

(There is a pause in the conversation as MIKE *and* SECRETARY *watch him narrowly. Finally* MIKE *speaks— with a note of false heartiness.)*

MIKE. Well, I guess I'll be running along—if nobody minds? (MIKE *picks up briefcase—repacks it, takes* SECRETARY *by the arm)* Can I give you a lift, Miss Logan?

(BRONK *shakes his head negatively—motions* MIKE *and* SECRETARY *stay put.)*

SECRETARY. You're wasting your time, Mr. Brannigan. Mr. MacCauley won't be back to the office tonight.

BRONK. He'll be here.

SECRETARY. What do you want with him anyway?

BRONK. *(Hand on switch in doorway)* I'm going to kill the little son of a bitch. *(He turns out all the lights but one at the desk. Gently he conducts* MIKE *and the* SECRETARY *downstage Right. Sits her with slight push in chair. Goes back and stands in doorway.)*

(There is a pause.)

MIKE. Have they ever named a sandwich after anyone —posthumously?

BRONK. Shaddup.

(Another pause. MIKE *raises his hand.)*
Yeah?

(MIKE *signals that he would like permission to cross and get his bottle.* BRONK *nods.* MIKE *crosses, gets the bottle and glass and returns to where he has been placed.*)

BRONK. I don't wanta peep outa either a ya. Not one peep— Shh! *(Crosses, gets behind door up Right, leading to inner office.)*

(The door opens and RITA *enters followed by* GEORGE. *She carries the Oscar.)*

GEORGE. Honest kid, this is crazy— We should have gone straight home.

RITA. Oh, no, Georgie! Not on a night like this! Anyhow, I want to see it there—on your desk— I want to look at it—gleaming there in the dark. Oh, Georgie, isn't it beautiful?

GEORGE. Yeah, it looks pretty good. I'm glad you like it, kid.

RITA. *(Sits on couch)* Oh, I do! I do! And I'm so proud of you. I just didn't dream you had a chance to win. But I wanted you to— I wanted you to so much.

GEORGE. *(Head on her lap)* Yeah, kid. I could tell you did.

RITA. I wanted you to win more than anything else in the world. And then you did.

GEORGE. Well it seemed like the least I could do for you. Besides, it was only another ten percent.

RITA. What?

GEORGE. Nothing— Now come on, kid. If you're so proud of me—make me know it!

RITA. Oh, baby doll! You'll know it! Will you ever just know it!

(At this point, BRONK *who can stand it any longer snaps on the lights.)*

MIKE. Okay, cut! I am a man of delicate sensibilities and—
RITA. Michael!
GEORGE. Miss Logan—

(She rises.)

BRONK. *(In doorway)* What about me—whatta 'bout *my* sensibilities!
RITA. Bronk!
BRONK. That's right, baby, I been waiting for ya. *(Slams door shut. Crosses Center.)*
RITA. *(To in front of* BRONK*)* Well, this certainly is a surprise. Does everybody know everybody? This is Michael Freeman, the playwright. And Miss Logan, Mr. MacCauley's secretary. And Georgie, this is Bronk. I'm sure you heard me speak of him. We were formerly married.
BRONK. *(Grabs her arm)* We're still married.
RITA. And Bronk, I don't think you've ever met Mr. MacCauley—
BRONK. No. I didn't have the pleasure. *(To desk; picks up Oscar; sits on desk, legs dangling)* But I been reading about him in the papers. And tonight I saw him on television. Honest, baby, when I saw him on the screen there —I didn't believe it. I said, "I don't believe it!" Rita shacked up with that little punk!
GEORGE. *(Crosses Left)* Mr. Brannigan, I must ask you to leave. Or I shall be compelled to call the studio police.
RITA. *(To Center)* That's right, Georgie, that's just what you do!
BRONK. Pal, you ain't calling nobody—
GEORGE. Miss Logan—would you please be good enough to call the police.
MIKE. I'm afraid the lines are all down.
BRONK. You know I came here I had the idea I was gonna break you in half. Now I see that ain't possible.
GEORGE. I'm very glad.

BRONK. Nah—he's already broken in half. *(Pushes
GEORGE to couch)* So I'm gonna break him in *quarters!*

RITA. Michael, aren't you going to do something?

MIKE. *(Has picked up exerciser once again. He tries it.
Nothing. Drops it under ledge Right)* I don't think so—
no— *(Crosses to door. Pours drink.)*

GEORGE. *(Rises)* Don't worry, kid, I was reading just
the other day where the small wiry chap can take the
bigger fellow every time.

BRONK. *(Tosses him onto the couch with butt of
Oscar)* Pipe down for a minute! I wanna talk to Rita!
You look great, baby, just like you always did. Come on
now how about a little kiss for old Bronk?

RITA. Keep away from me!

GEORGE. *(Rises; grabs BRONK's arms)* Yes. You take
your hands off her!

BRONK. *(Tosses him back onto the couch)* I'll get to you
in a minute. *(Crosses to desk.)*

MIKE. *(Pulls himself together, puts down his drink and
crosses to BRONK)* Okay, Brannigan, here goes nothing.
(He swings wildly and rapidly lands a right to the body)

(BRONK, however, does not bat an eye.)

(Apologetically to group) I saw it in a movie once— I always wanted to try it.

BRONK. You got it wrong, Mister, what you saw was this—

(BRONK *hits* MIKE *in the solar plexus with a right.* MIKE
crumples, bends jack-knifed. BRONK *gives him slight
push on the head and* MIKE *stretches out on floor
near chair down Right.* SECRETARY *works over his
limp form during the following.)*

RITA. *(Crosses to desk)* Bronk, you've just absolutely
flipped your lid again.

BRONK. I don't know what it is about you, baby. Sometimes you make me mad. Real mad. But I don't care. For
some reason I want you to come back to me.

RITA. *(At desk)* You really don't mean that—it's just,

now that Spring Training is over, you don't know what to do with yourself—

BRONK. Maybe. But I know what to do with you, remember? *(Grabs her.)*

RITA. Bronk! I don't love you!

BRONK. *(Faces* GEORGE) I suppose you love that little punk!

RITA. That's right! I love that little punk!

GEORGE. That's right!

BRONK. Okay. We'll see how much. We'll make a little deal. Either you come back to me or I kill him—right now with my bare hands—

RITA. Bronk, you'll never get away with this!

BRONK. *(Flips* GEORGE *upstage)* I'll get away with it all right. You ever hear of the *unwritten law?* I'm still married to her. You broke up my happy home. I got every right to kill you. Besides—who's gonna know. Rita's the only witness—and a wife can't testify against her husband. Okay, baby, you got a choice—do I kill him or do you come back— Make up your mind or I break him in little pieces—

RITA. Georgie, what should I do?

BRONK. *(To* GEORGE) Little *tiny* pieces. *(Shakes him. He tosses him over to the couch again. To* RITA) Okay, now, that's how it is. I move back in tonight—

RITA. Oh, no, Bronk, that just isn't possible. What we'll do—we'll start the new arrangement—the first of next week—

BRONK. *The first of next week? (Crosses to her.)*

RITA. Yes. Of course. It'll take me a little time. I mean if you're going to move back and everything. I have to clean out closets and the laundry with the clean sheets comes back Tuesday. So why don't we say next Tuesday —we could start next Tuesday—

BRONK. Baby—this is Bronko— *(He grabs her and begins making violent love to her.)*

GEORGE. (GEORGE *can't stand it. He flings himself at* BRONK) Now, take your hands off her.

(BRONK'S *patience is exhausted. He turns and slaps* GEORGE—*who falls to the couch.*)

Irving!

(IRVING *materializes in a spotlight down Left in front of the tormentor and moves into the room to down Left.*)

IRVING. Dear boy!

GEORGE. *(To Right Center)* Irving! You're here!

IRVING. At your beck and call. Any hour of the night or day. I ask you, does Charlie Feldman give such service?

RITA. Sneaky! What are you doing here?

IRVING. LaSalle Service. And now then, my dearest boy, what is your pleasure?

BRONK. What's this, another little punk?

GEORGE. All my life I've been pushed around by—big—*football players*—like him. Once—*just once*—I'd like to be able to do something about it— Can you fix it, Irving?

IRVING. Do you remember dear Spencer Tracy in an amusing little film called BAD DAY AT BLACK ROCK?

GEORGE. *(Right Center)* The judo scene?

IRVING. The high point of the picture!

BRONK. What the hell are you two guys talking about?

IRVING. If you like, dear boy, I believe this can be BAD DAY AT BLACK ROCK all over again—

GEORGE. I like—

(IRVING *holds out his hand.* GEORGE *shakes it.*)

IRVING. Very well, so be it. Congratulations.

BRONK. Okay, you two guys. Blow. Me and Rita got things to do.

(BRONK *starts to grab* RITA *again—but he is stopped by* GEORGE'S *sudden, new, ice-cold voice.*)

GEORGE. Hey, kid, stand well back—

RITA. *(Breaking away from* BRONK) George, be careful!

GEORGE. Well back—

(Very calmly GEORGE goes up to BRONK and slaps him across the face—with the front and then the back of his hand—movie style. BRONK lunges at him. GEORGE, barely moving, deftly catches BRONK's arm and flips over his shoulder. BRONK comes crashing to the floor on the other side of the room.)

IRVING. Go, man, go, go, go.

(BRONK *pulls himself together and charges again. There follows the damndest fight you ever saw. Effortlessly,* GEORGE *tosses* BRONK *from one end of the room to the other. A beautifully executed series of flips.)*

RITA. *(With wide-eyed admiration)* George, you're so wiry!
SECRETARY. Kick him. Mr. MacCauley, kick him!
GEORGE. Musclebound!
BRONK. I'm gonna kill you—

(With one last, heroic effort BRONK *lunges again. For a moment there is a fierce tangle of arms and legs and then* BRONK *is flying out the window. A loud CRASH is heard.)*

GEORGE. *(He's not even breathing hard)* Sorry, kid. He had it coming.
RITA. *(Flinging herself into his arms)* Georgie!

(They clinch.)

MIKE. *(Staggers to the window joining* IRVING *and* SECRETARY *who are peering out)* I knew damn well I shouldn't have parked my car down there. What are you going to do with him?

IRVING. If it were up to me I should leave him there indefinitely. However, Good Samaritanwise I fear the only thing to do is gather him up and take him to the hospital.

GEORGE. He's absolutely right. Poor Mr. Brannigan.

Come on, kid—we'll take your car. *(Crosses up Right Center.)*

(MIKE *stretches out on the couch.*)

IRVING. What about you, dear Michael. Can we drop you?

MIKE. I've already been dropped, thanks— *(Reclines on couch.)*

SECRETARY. But what are you going to do, Mr. Freeman?

MIKE. I am going to lie here, Miss Logan, and soon the birds will come over and cover me with leaves. Meanwhile, I suggest you force whisky down my throat.

IRVING. Dear boy— Come along, children. And George, may I tell you what a pleasure it is to own ninety per cent of such a talented, wealthy, two-fisted, hard-punching, Academy Award winning, pet, lover, adventurer, etcetera, etcetera—good-night.

(As they exit—

BLACKOUT

ACT THREE

SCENE II

SCENE: *Office. Next morning.*

MIKE *is discovered on couch, jacket covering him as lights dim up.*

GEORGE. *(Enters up Right carrying Oscar and box)* Mike— I'm glad you're here, Mike— I stopped by your house and you weren't there. Get up, Mike, it's nine o'clock.

MIKE. A.M. or P.M.?

GEORGE. Look, Mike, I'm leaving town this morning. I'm in kind of a hurry—but I had to see you for a minute —before I leave—

MIKE. *(Sits up)* What's the matter, kid? Where are you running to?

GEORGE. Brooklyn, Mike. Brooklyn. I got to get out of Hollywood before it's too late.

MIKE. I don't know what the hell you're talking about. You just won the Oscar for the best screenplay of the year and—

GEORGE. No. No, I didn't. *(Crosses Right)* Not really. Not the way you think I did, anyway. It was all a fake. *(Puts Oscar on ledge)* A big fake. And I just feel terrible about it. I didn't do anything at all. I mean—all *I* did was—

MIKE. I know what you did. I saw the picture.

GEORGE. *(Puts box on desk. Crosses and sits down Right)* That's what I mean! You had this wonderful play about homosexuals and prostitutes and exerything! And I just ruined it! I ruin everything I touch. That's why I have to talk to you. Mike, do you remember the first year we met. That day last year—back in New York when I came to interview Rita?

MIKE. *(Crosses down Center)* Sure.

GEORGE. Well, that's when it all began! Irving LaSalle —he's the one! It's all his fault! He's not even *human!*

MIKE. I know. He's an agent.

GEORGE. He's worse than that, Mike. Much worse. He —he can do *anything! Anything!* He can get you anything you want in the world for ten per cent of your soul— What's the matter, Mike?

MIKE. *(Crosses up Right Center; takes bottle)* Nothing. Nothing at all. It's just that I could swear I heard you say "ten per cent of your soul."

GEORGE. That's what I did say. For each wish. There's no written agreement of course. With Irving a handshake is sufficient.

MIKE. I seem to be having enormous difficulty following this conversation. *(Drinks whisky)* It has the same

ACT III   WILL SUCCESS SPOIL ROCK HUNTER?   65

number of calories as orange juice. Exactly. Are you trying to tell me Irving LaSalle is the devil or something?

GEORGE. I don't think he's actually the devil. As a matter of fact—I asked him once. Point blank. I said: *"Are you?"* And he said: "Oh, no, dear boy. Nothing so exalted as that. I am merely the head of the Literary Department. You *do* believe me, don't you, Mike?

MIKE. Believe you? You know something? I think you're out of your goddamn mind. *(Crosses up Right Center; puts back bottle.)*

GEORGE. Mike—you know *me!* *(Rists; crosses Left)* You know I can't write a movie or win an Oscar or do anything! But I did! *(To Right Center)* Because Irving fixed it for me. Anything I wanted. It cost me ten per cent for each wish. Of course it's true! *(To Left Center)* I mean how do you think I beat up Bronk Brannigan? *(To down Left)* Suddenly it was BAD DAY AT BLACK ROCK and the next thing I knew—there was Mr. Brannigan—flying out the window! He's at the Cedars of Lebanon Hospital right now— I tell you, Mike, you just can't believe how much I hate myself. Ever since this whole thing started I've just done one terrible thing after another. That's why I'm getting out of here. I have to get out of Hollywood while I still have ten percent left!

MIKE. *(Crosses down Right; sits)* Ten percent left? What the hell did you do with the other ninety?

GEORGE. *(Crosses up to desk)* Well, it's kind of hard to keep track of. First of all there was the million dollars he gave me and then Rita being in love with me and then all that poet, lover, adventurer business. *(To Left Center)* Mr. LaSalle was certainly right about *that!* That's one ten per cent that I just don't regret at all! *(To down Left)* Then I wished for the story that day at the meeting. *(To Center)* You remember. You were there. Then the Oscar and then the fight with Mr. Brannigan.

MIKE. That's still only sixty percent.

GEORGE. I know. But there were a couple of other little things. I'm embarrassed to tell you. It's just that I could never resist showing off. That's all I am! Just a big show off! Especially in front of Rita!

MIKE. *(Rises)* What are you talking about?

GEORGE. You remember that day at the Tennis Club—when Charlie Lederer and I beat Segura and Herbie Flam—only we played handcuffed together?

MIKE. Okay—seventy per cent—

GEORGE. And then there was this one other little thing—Well, you know, her picture. She wasn't going to get the part— They wanted Grace Kelly—

(MIKE *looks genuinely startled.*)

You think it was *easy* for Mr. LaSalle? That *Prince*— The *Zoo*— Pictures on stamps—shlepping Rita Gam halfway round the world— You never saw such a Federal case!

(MIKE *drinks from bottle.*)

And there's one more thing. *(Crosses to desk)* I feel kind of funny about it. That's why I came this morning. That's why I had to tell you the whole truth so you'd understand.

MIKE. Understand what, George?

GEORGE. *(Has picked up the carboard box tied with a string. Holding it in his hand)* This.

MIKE. *(Curiously)* What is it?

GEORGE. It's a present for you.

MIKE. What the hell are you talking about?

GEORGE. It's kind of a going-away present. I mean you're the only friend I've got out here. And you were so nice about everything. And I do feel just awful about how I ruined your play. So here—take it Mike. *(Hands him box.)*

MIKE. Well, in the words of the immortal Harry Kaye, "I'm touched." It's very nice of you— I certainly appreciate it. *(By this time he has opened the box)* What the hell is this? *(Looks at script.)*

GEORGE. *(Shyly)* The Pulitzer Prize Play for 1958. By Michael Freeman.

MIKE. The Pulitzer Prize Play for 1958! By Michael Freeman?

GEORGE. Neatly typed. With six carbons. *(Takes box from* MIKE*)* And Irving said to tell you that these are three sets of rewrites. *(Parroting* IRVING*)* You're supposed to put one set in New Haven, one in Boston, and this one in Philadelphia. *(Returns box.)*

(MIKE *looks at the script aghast. For once he is speechless. Moves away.)*

I hope you're not mad or anything, Mike. But you seemed to be having so much trouble writing your new play. And I remember how you said the second one is always the hardest. So I thought you'd like it.

MIKE. *(Crosses to Center)* You spent another ten per cent of your soul to get me a new play?

GEORGE. That's right, Mike. You do like it don't you,

MIKE. This is really going to win the Pulitzer Prize for 1958?

GEORGE. Oh, yes— Irving promised. *(Tosses box on couch. Pause)* What's the matter Mike?

MIKE. *(Sits on couch)* Georgie, even if I did believe you, I couldn't take this thing.

GEORGE. *(Crosses up to couch)* Why not Mike, it's *my* ten percent. It won't cost *you* anything.

MIKE. That's where you're wrong, George. The Pulitzer Prize, huh?

GEORGE. That's right. *(Crosses up Left)* Oh, it's going to be a big hit. I wasn't going to tell you—it was supposed to be a little extra surprise but 20th Century Fox is going to buy it *for eight hundred thousand dollars! (To Center)* You do believe me, don't you, Mike?

MIKE. *(Rises; crosses Right)* I believe you. I really believe you. Georgie—a wonderful thing just happened— *(To Left Center)* Just happened right this second. You know there have been plenty of times in the last two years when I wished I could just push a button or something and there my new play would be—all neatly typed. With six carbons. And three sets of rewrites for New Haven, Boston, and Philadelphia. *(To Center)* And now that I got it— I suddenly realize I don't want it. That's a wonderful thing. You just gave me a present, Georgie. The best damn present I ever had.

GEORGE. I don't understand, Mike.

MIKE. You made me realize I'm a *writer*, Georgie. A *writer*. I got this thing in my hand and I suddenly knew I wasn't going to use it. I *couldn't* use it. I suddenly realized I got too much pride—professional pride—if you want to call it that—to stick my name on something I didn't write. You did a great thing for me—a great thing. *(Shakes hands)* Thanks for the present, George. Thanks a lot. But no thanks. Look, you better get going. You'll miss your plane.

GEORGE. *(Crosses Right; turns)* Yeah. I've got to hurry. I've got to get out of here before it's too late. You see, Irving can't touch me until he gets the whole hundred percent, but I only have ten percent left. And if he gets that I'm gone. Rita was still asleep when I left so I left her a note. I told her she should try to forget me. That it's all for the best. But she probably won't be able to. I mean she's like bewitched. But at least she still has her work. She's right in the middle of shooting THE GIRL FROM VALLEY FORGE.

MIKE. What the hell is she *playing*—Martha Washington?

GEORGE. No. It's really very interesting. Rita plays this tavern-keeper's daughter who runs away and joins Washington's army—disguised as a boy—

MIKE. That's not interesting. That's remarkable.

(At this point RITA *appears up Right. She is dressed in travelling clothes.)*

RITA. Georgie!

GEORGE. Kid! What are you doing here?

RITA. *(Crosses to Center)* Oh, Georgie, I'm so glad I found you—when I got your note I just cried and cried— I couldn't stop. *(Embraces him.)*

GEORGE. *(Breaks embrace)* I'm sorry it's got to be this way kid—but that's life. Here today, gone tomorrow—

RITA. For a minute I felt all lost. I didn't know what to do— Then I decided. I just called the studio and I told them.

MIKE. *(To down Right)* Told them what, Rita?

RITA. Oh, hello Michael. I just told them how I'm quitting pictures. I decided I'm going to Brooklyn with Georgie. We'll live with his aunt. Isn't that divoon!

MIKE. Divoon. Divoon.

GEORGE. Kid—I can't let you do this!

RITA. Oh, Georgie, you will let me go with you, won't you, doll baby? I can't live without you, you know that. And I just can wait to meet Aunt Jessie. I *can* come with you, can't I, Georgie?

(They melt into each other's arms, kiss.)

MIKE. Hey, George, have you ever thought of running for President?

HARRY. *(An irate* HARRY *comes storming in up Right. With ironic sweetness)* Hello, Young Lovers! Drop dead.

(GEORGE *and* RITA *break embrace. He is upstage; she has a hand on his shoulder.)*

RITA. Hello, Harry.

GEORGE. Good morning, Mr. Kaye—

HARRY. My boy. Mr. Vice President. What are you trying to do to me? I'm an old man. A naturalized citizen. I treated you like a son—and you—right in the middle of THE GIRL FROM VALLEY FORGE—you kidnap the broad! I tell you one thing! This broad walks off this picture and she's through! Washed up! She never works in this industry again! Right this minute, on Stage Eleven —twenty thousand tons of real snow—*melting*— *(His voice breaks with emotion)* Mr. Lurman—for thirty-two years the head of my special effects—he comes to me on bended knee. "Harry," he says, "I beg of you—use cornflakes like everybody else!" "No," I told him. "For this little lady, nothing but the best! Real snow!" "But

Harry," he says, "cornflakes don't melt!" But I won't listen. No, I had faith in my artist! Real snow! Sand bags are holding back the floods! *(The tears are streaming down his face. He pulls himself together, strides off up Right.)*

RITA. *(Calling after him)* I don't care! *(She bursts into tears)* I love you, Georgie! That's all I care about!

IRVING. *(Appearing up Right and crossing down Right)* Gentlemen! And the divine Rita! How is everyone this glorious morning?

MIKE. The spring thaws have set in. Men and boats needed on Stage Eleven. *(Crosses up Left; sits.)*

GEORGE. *(Crosses to* IRVING*)* Irving, I got to talk to you. I can't let Rita do this. She's ruining her whole career—her whole life. Irving, I've got to make her stop being in love with me. I can still do that—can't I Irving?

IRVING. Of course. However, permit me to remind you that this is your last ten per cent. And, I may say, the only ten per cent that really counts.

GEORGE. I don't care about me. I love her— I really love her—and that's what I want to do—all right?

IRVING. Very well, so be it.

(They shake. There is a pause while MIKE, GEORGE *and* IRVING *turn to watch* RITA. *She has a peculiar, half-puzzled expression on her face.)*

RITA. *(After a moment)* Michael—what time is it?

MIKE. Must be about ten-thirty—

RITA. Ten-thirty! Golly, I'm late! I've got to get to the studio. Goodbye, Michael—goodbye, Sneaky— Oh, yes— Goodbye, Mr. Klein! *(She exits up Right.)*

GEORGE. Thanks, Irving.

IRVING. A pleasure, dear boy.

GEORGE. Well, what happens now? *(Sits on couch.)*

IRVING. *(Crosses to Right Center)* Now, I'm afraid we've come to the end of the road. The string, shall we say, has run out. The game is over.

MIKE. *(Rises; to Left Center)* Irving, I'm not going to let you take George.

IRVING. *(To up Right Center)* I beg your pardon, dear boy.

MIKE. I'm not going to let you take George.

IRVING. How may I ask do you propose to stop me?

MIKE. Now, Irving, I bet there's a way. *(To Right Center)* Think about it for a minute. Let that wild free agent's imagination of yours grapple with the problem—

IRVING. Ah! I'm not quite sure I see what you have on your mind—

MIKE. Of course you do. A LaSalle client can do anything, Irving. We all know that.

IRVING. Michael, if you are really serious about this, I suppose we could work out something.

MIKE. I imagined we could.

GEORGE. Mike, you don't know what you're doing—

MIKE. Sure I do. I know exactly what I'm doing—

IRVING. This is, you understand a rather special case, however—

MIKE. Come off it, Irving. You'd rather have me than him, wouldn't you? I mean, how many Pulitzer Prize winners you got down there, anyway?

IRVING. A few. As a matter of fact I imagine you would find it a rather congenial bunch.

MIKE. Okay. Let's talk turkey.

IRVING. Very well, under the circumstances the very best I can do is the following. I can arrange for you to take over George's contract at ninety per cent.

GEORGE. Don't do it. I can't let you.

MIKE. Forget it kid. You got a deal, Irving?

IRVING. Deal. Congratulations. And permit me to tell you what an honor and pleasure it is to own ninety per cent of such a great-hearted humanitarian. George, dear boy, although you are no longer a LaSalle client, common courtesy demands that I place my car and chauffeur outside at your disposal. He will be more than happy to drive you to the bus station.

GEORGE. Mike, I don't understand. *(Backs)* How could

you go ahead and do a thing like this for me— I mean ninety per cent—

MIKE. Think nothing of it. Think nothing of it. It couldn't matter less.

IRVING. *(To Left Center)* Michael, aren't you taking a rather cavalier attitude?

MIKE. Irving, you've been had. You've been done. You blew the deal, kid. The William Morris office could of handled this one much better than you did.

IRVING. Michael, I do not understand.

MIKE. I shall explain. Georgie boy you lost altogether. Right? And me you will never get. So—I would say— you blew the deal.

IRVING. What makes you think I'll never get you, Michael?

MIKE. Irving, you can't touch me until you get the whole hundred percent, and that you'll never get. I mean what have you got to tempt me with? A million dollars? I got a million dollars—or damn near—and I can earn all I want in pictures any time I want to. Girls? Irving, I do pretty well in that department on my own. I have no desire to fight football players, win Oscars, restore the bosom, or beat Herbie Flam. The only place you could touch me is as a writer, with a new play. But I just found out—ten minutes ago—that in that particular area I'm not for sale. *(He lifts the script out of the box)* Georgie's little present, recognize it?

IRVING. Of course. A distinguished play. A record movie sale. And Buddy Adler will personally produce the picture.

MIKE. *(Begins to tear the srript into pieces. Little tiny pieces)* Never happen, Irving, never happen. Him you don't get. Me you don't get. And I have the damndest feeling you don't even get Rock Hunter. Whoever the hell he may be.

IRVING. Dear Michael—

MIKE. Scram, Irving. Blow. Get lost.

IRVING. Very well. Goodbye Michael. And George—as far as I'm concerned you can *walk* to the bus station.

(IRVING *picks up* GEORGE'S *Oscar and with almost a small boy's "So there!" expression, puts it under his arm and exits up Right.*)

MIKE. *(Begins triumphantly to toss torn pieces of paper into the air. Toss)* The Pulitzer Prize!
GEORGE. The re-writes for New Haven! *(Toss.)*
MIKE. The re-writes for Philadelphia. *(Toss.)*
(They both regard the falling pieces of paper.)
Remind you of anything, Georgie? Snow! *(He is continuing to toss handfuls of paper into the air.)*
GEORGE. *(Suddenly it does)* Yeah! That's right.
MIKE. What month is this?
GEORGE. March.
MIKE. We still got a chance for some snow in New York. The blizzard of '88 was in March. Look, Georgie, we take a plane and we can be in New York tomorrow! In time for the snowstorm! The only thing I need is my clothes—

(GEORGE *picks up his suitcase.*)
(MIKE *starts—then stops himself*) I don't need my clothes. The hell with my clothes. I don't need anything. I'm a writer, Georgie, a writer. If you want to be a writer you don't have to wish for it—you just sit down at the typewriter and do it. You know what I mean.

GEORGE. I guess so. Actually, the only thing I ever wrote was this one article I called it "WILL SUCCESS SPOIL ROCK HUNTER?" Actually, it was quite well received for what it was—

(MIKE *is hustling him out as*

THE CURTAIN FALLS

WILL SUCCESS SPOIL ROCK HUNTER?

PROPS

ACT ONE

Mantelpiece:
Cigarette lighter—DSR
Dog
Clock
Bowl of flowers
Teddy bear (floor) LSR
Stork—USR
Stool—SR
One box (closed) USR against door
Box of flowers R of table

On table SR:
Basket of fruit
Matches
Cigarettes
Ash tray
Radio
Telephone with extension
Hand towel
Massage kit—2 bottles—hand towel

Box on floor to L of table
Pink dog under table
Box under table
End table under electric bracket
Bowl of flowers
Ash tray
6 film magazines

Chair in front of table
Sofa SL with green pillow
Table, back of sofa
5 Martini glasses, ash tray, cigarettes, matches
Bottles of gin
Martini mixer
Picture—back of table SR
Pencil for GEORGE MACCAULEY—SL
Note book for GEORGE MACCAULEY—SL
Cigar for HARRY KAYE—SL
Books in bookcase
Chair USL

On bookcase:
Ice bucket
Mixer
Martini mixer, ice cubes
Bottle of Dubonnet wine
Bottle Vermouth
Bottle gin
Corks
Bottles

Valence box with drapes
2 rugs
Fireplace

ACT TWO—Office

Outer office of Secretary:
Table USR
Picture of RITA MARLOWE above table L
Lamp on US table
Door has the following lettering: "RITA MARLOWE PRODUCTIONS." "GEO. MACCAULEY—VICE PRES."
Secretary desk DS

Following items are on the desk:
Telephone
Ash tray

PROPS

Cigarettes
Matches
Script
Note book
Pencil
Elbow lamp

Secretary chair is set with back to audience

Inner office:
Chair DSR
Ash tray—pencil—notebook on ledge DSR
Bookcase with 8 tiers of books SRC
Drawer at bottom of bookcase
Large plant in flower pot RC
Couch with ledge on Right of it
Window curtains, removable windows (also taped windows re "Brannigan")—SC
Transparent figurine case with 4 ebony figurines—SC
Large picture of RITA MARLOWE USL

ARC desk SL upon which is the following:
Aspirin
Glass
Memo-calendar
Ash tray
Telephone
Paper
Pen and pencil desk set
Ebony box containing cigarettes and matches

Red floor mat (double sectioned) covers entire floor area
8-tiered bookshelf above desk USL
One tier is divided thusly: one side plant; other side Gigure modern head
Typewriter on retractable wall board DSL
Picture of RITA MARLOWE above typewriter DSL
Sword (Joan of Arc), silver finish
Mattress—outside of window—used to break BRONK'S fall

WILL SUCCESS SPOIL ROCK HUNTER?

FURNITURE AND PROPS

2 special #18 SPT de-luxe mats
Black cigarette box
Black double pen base (dummy pen)
Black calendar pad
Black hexagonal ash tray
Black round waste basket
2 ash trays
Special desk pad, black leather
Side chair, magnesium-gold finish covered in pigskin tile
Arm chair, black finish white nylon cord seat and back
Swivel arm chair, walnut base covered in black leather
    and black and white fabric
3 modern lamps
Goose neck
Books
African or pre-Columbian sculpture
Indian dolls
3 picture frames
9 framed "awards"
2 plants—tropical ivy
6 vases

Some of this is included on other prop list

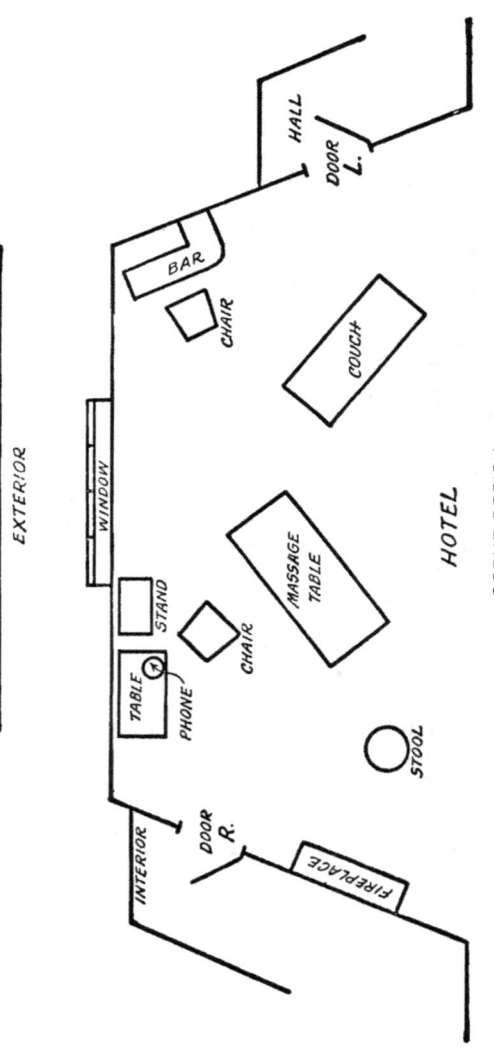

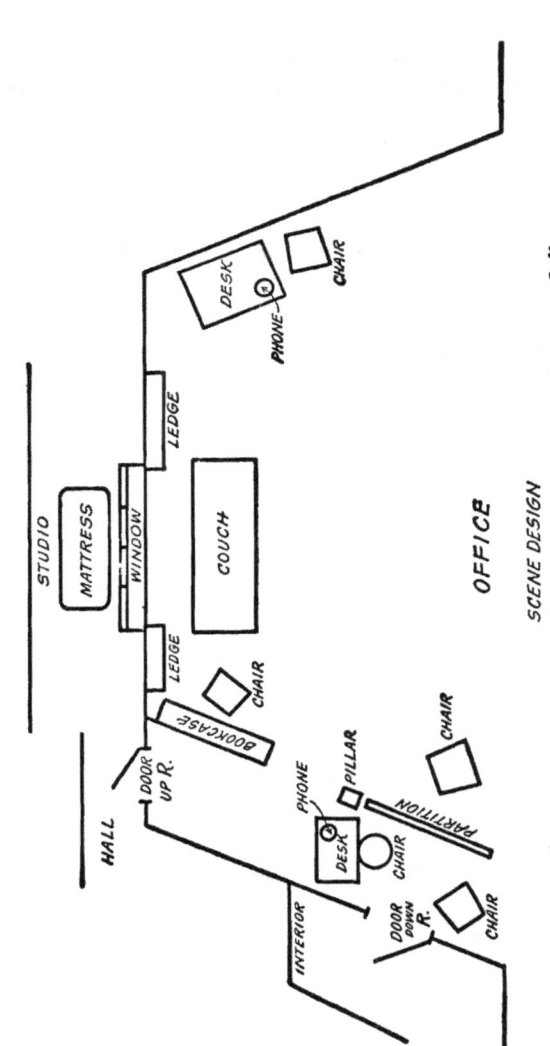

"WILL SUCCESS SPOIL ROCK HUNTER?"

SCENE DESIGN

MUSIC USE NOTE

Licensees are solely responsible for obtaining formal written permission from copyright owners to use copyrighted music in the performance of this play and are strongly cautioned to do so. If no such permission is obtained by the licensee, then the licensee must use only original music that the licensee owns and controls. Licensees are solely responsible and liable for all music clearances and shall indemnify the copyright owners of the play(s) and their licensing agent, Samuel French, against any costs, expenses, losses and liabilities arising from the use of music by licensees. Please contact the appropriate music licensing authority in your territory for the rights to any incidental music.

IMPORTANT BILLING AND CREDIT REQUIREMENTS

If you have obtained performance rights to this title, please refer to your licensing agreement for important billing and credit requirements.

www.ingramcontent.com/pod-product-compliance
Lightning Source LLC
Chambersburg PA
CBHW072019290426
44109CB00018B/2284